Master Dating®: How to Meet & Attract Quality Men!

By
Felicia Rose Adler

BLUE SKY MARKETING INC.
PO Box 21583-S, St. Paul, MN 55121 USA

Edited by Virginia Iorio
Cover design by Michelle Hinko
Illustrated by Angela Fernandez
Inside book designed by Paula Roth

Printed in the United States of America

Published by:
BLUE SKY MARKETING INC.
PO Box 21583-S
St. Paul, MN 55121 USA
(651) 456-5602 / 800-444-5450
SAN 263-9394

Library of Congress Cataloging-in-Publication Data
Adler, Felicia Rose, 1965-
Master dating: how to meet & attract quality men! / by Felicia Rose Adler.
p. cm.
Includes bibliographical references.
ISBN 0-911493-24-7 (alk. paper)
1. Dating (Social customs) 2. Man-woman relationships. I. Title.
HQ801.A5146 1999
646.7'7—dc21

98-50194
CIP

8 7 6 5 4 3 2 1

Dedication

I dedicate this book to my mother, Jane Adler, a woman of courage, integrity, strength and limitless love who makes a powerful positive impact on everyone she meets. Those of us who have the good fortune of being on the receiving end of her charms are the lucky ones!

Table of Contents

Acknowledgments

As a first-time author, I can tell you this: The author is only one member of a team of people who create a successful book, and any book is only as great as the sum of all of its parts (team members). I wish I could put the name of every member of this book's team on the front cover next to mine.

I find myself wishing I had kept better track of all of those parts. I am now greatly concerned that I will leave out many people who deserve to be recognized. If you know me, you probably belong here.

First and foremost, I must say THANKS, MOM. Thank you most for teaching me the meaning of unconditional love, a lesson you teach ongoingly with your actions. I know that I can always depend on you and your love; you have never let me down. Thank you for "always knowing I could do it," though it would have been okay to *act* surprised when I actually did.

To my pop, "Taxi" Bob Adler, thank you for showing my mom what that kind of love (unconditional) feels like. And for taking such good care of both of us. Thank you for being such a great example of a quality man.

Thank you to my incredible friend Chelsea Fisher. For propping me up, holding me up and occasionally picking me up from a "huddled mass" on the floor. Your insight, patience and sense of humor have made such a difference in my life.

Next, my perfect publisher. Thank you, Vic Spadaccini of Blue Sky Marketing, for being smart enough (or crazy enough) to see my and this book's potential. Thank you also for investing your time, confidence, expertise and money in my book. I know that you and I will have a long and prosperous relationship. You are a wonderful person and an incredibly smart businessman!

My father, David Lee Hanan, is where I get my ability to sell ice to the Eskimos. Thank you for telling me at a very early age, "Felicia, I know you. You can do anything you set your mind to!" I believed you.

I would like to thank Kevin Klein for fixing my wagon on a regular basis (except that last time). You are a genius. You have deeply impacted my life.

There are a number of people who were instrumental in having this book come to fruition. A special thank-you to these most important people. This is my support team:

Cyndi DeClerck, you make my business fly. Thank you for acting as *"that"* glue in so many ways. You are a dear friend. You are irreplaceable.

Angela Fernandez, the illustrator of this book. You are an incredible artist with a great sense of humor. You will be a huge success!

Stacey Shur McKernan, you are such a huge part of who I am, and I'm glad of it! I love you and your family. Hi, Tim and Danielle.

Cat Williford, to me you are a teacher, a healer and a friend. Thank you for always "getting" me, and then explaining me to me.

Michelle Hinko, the incredible artist for the cover of this book and a dear friend. Thank you for your hard work and patience. You are the best!

Paula Roth, the artist who painstakenly formatted this book. Thank you for working so diligently to do the thankless job of putting order to my disordered manuscript. You did a fabulous job!

Kim Reaver, wherever you are (please contact me). I do not think I would have made it to age 14 without you. You are a courageous, unique, pure, incredible, beautiful and benevolent (angel) soul. I miss you.

The following list of people are the readers of my manuscript. I respect these people and their opinions to the utmost degree. Thank you for giving of your time, energy, brilliance and heart. Each of you added your own unique touch and bettered this book greatly. In alphabetical order:

The magnificent Hallie Dash, the amazing Cyndi DeClerck, the talented Angela Fernandez, the brilliant Tiffany Fisher, the fantastic Noal Hebert, the wonderful Dena Honig, the incredible Joy Kirschenbaum, the fabulous Tussanee Luebbers, the marvelous Deb McGougan, the remarkable Kristina Reed, the sharp Ellen Reid, the terrific Lauren Stratton, and Rhoda Walsh, who is class personified.

Next I wish to thank my editors:

Elaine Holifield, thank you not only for working so diligently on editing the manuscript, but also for fixing so many of the pieces leading up to it. You are an incredible woman with a huge heart and a laugh to match.

Virginia Iorio, I feel like I should call you "SUPER EDITOR": Able to change my book without hurting my feelings! Able to see incorrect details that are not normally visible to the human eye. You are so great!

Now I want to mention four incredible teacher/mentors:

Ms. Nancy Curry, my 5th and 6th grade teacher (please contact me), for teaching me who I am and what I'm capable of. She is the kind of teacher who strives to impact the lives of her students, and she uses her love and creativity to do so.

Mr. Frank Kovac—without the encouragement of this teacher I wouldn't have enough confidence to write a good sentence, let alone a book. He would return my essays with a hundred red marks and accolades that took up as much space as my essay. Oh, and a "B+"! He also heroically jumped in to help edit this book. What a guy!

Sherri Cannon, my public speaking mentor. You make a difference in all that you do and say. You teach as much with your actions as with your words.

Chellie Campbell, and her financial stress reduction workshop. What you teach is so valuable and needed. You get a lot of credit for the success of this book. You are a brilliant and powerful soul.

Acknowledgements

I want to recognize the following special people as having greatly impacted my life, each in their own special way. They are listed in no particular order:

JoJo Larsen, Leah Lindberg, Ofra Peters, Berneice Seminaio, Maria Macias, Loretta and Stan Shur, Tony Shur (computer whiz), Frankie McKernan (whiz), Patty De Dominic, Karen Stupel, Tracey Purdum, John Todt, Sam Horn, Cherri Grimm, Susan Jeffers, Dottie Walters, Mark Victor Hansen, Jack Canfield, James Malenchak, Jill Spiegel, Sheri Moses, Danette Lindeman, Mike Levin, Jacob Spielman, and Curt Alexander and his friends and family, especially his magnificent mother, Marlene Alexander (I think of you and your lessons often).

To my family, your love and support make me feel that I have a foundation. You are where I come from. With this thank-you I send a huge hug.

Extra special recognition to Jack, Elayne, Elizabeth, Heather and Lily Greenberg and Joy Kirschenbaum. Thank you to the Hanans, including Gido and Sido (Jack and Mildred Hanan), Uncle Joe and Aunt Marilyn, Uncle Marty, Aunt Jackie and Stacey too! Frankie, Joyce, Ruthie and Rosie. Jack, Angel, Joe and Rachel and also Mark. Of course my brother John, Debbie, David and Catie. My dad David Lee and Karen, Natalie and Mitch. The rest of the Greenbergs, Aunt Joy, Uncle Ralph, Arnie, Nancy, Hailey and Harrison. The Kirschenbaums, a big kiss to Aunt Carole, Uncle Jay, Jack and Henri, Mark and Crissie. The Jacob family, Susie, Freddie, Joy, Melissa and Elana. The Ocevedos, Varin, Rudy, Joe and Dana. The Yarkins, Dawn, Richard, and Makayla. And Kestinbaums, Rita, Ronald, Sammy, Louie, and Carol. ***Whew!***

I thank the following people for their dependably positive energy, wisdom, support for me and this book, and for always sharing a big smile. Listed in the order you appear in my Day-Timer:

Aline Lapierre, Anne Otoide, Brenda Guttman, Bryan Russo, Chris Whitfield, Cyndi Brown, Cheryl Lutjen, Caitlin Cross-Barnett, Celine Lass, Carmen Diamond, Kristina Reed, Donna Mosada, Dena Honig, Gail Fraker, Judith Ross, John Crites, John Jarrel, John Walker, Kai Bravo, Karen Morino, Katherine Chrisman, Kari Reeser, Lauren Stratton, Liz Segul, Laurie Pessel, Letty Reeser, Loretta Dash, Lissa Caruth, the French family, Marie Sterling, Melody Coles and Art too, Nancy Bunn, Nora Wolin, Patricia Hodgeman, Pam Hassen, Paula Borchardt, Reza Kounevard, Ruby Juce, Sharon Homich, Sharon Weiss, Shauna Krikorian, Susan Fransblau, Victor Osaka, Willie Herrera and Wendy James.

Introduction

This book is chock-full of advice on how to meet and attract the kind of quality man you want. I will take it a step further by showing you how to situate yourself so that you end up sitting across the table sharing a meal and some conversation with him.

If you are currently dissatisfied with your love life for any reason, this book has the answer. Whether you haven't had a date in years, or you are fending off Mr. Wrong daily, the solutions to your dilemma will be found within these pages. For some of you each page will be full of "Ah-Ha!s" and light bulbs. Others may find one particular concept that changes everything. Whether you need a whole new mindset or just that one missing link for success, this book has every angle of dating covered from every angle.

The first question women always ask me is, "Where can I meet men?" My response is, "Where *can't* you meet men?" They are everywhere we normally go. You could run into the man you're looking for at the bank, the market, the post office, the gas station, anywhere. I say the question is not *where*, it's HOW!

This book will teach you how to turn a chance meeting (or sighting) into a date. We will go over a multitude of possible situations and scenarios with specific advice on how to deal with each. We'll talk about many places and opportunities, ways and means. By the time we're through, you will not only feel hopeful, but actually excited about the idea of dating.

Finding "The One"

We must all realize that we already know the men that we know. Let me explain. You have a circle of people who you know. Those people have a circle of people who they know. Unless you are opposed to being set up, you have probably already figured out that none of the men you currently have access to is "The One" for you.

The purpose of this book is to create options in your love life. I am not saying that you should try to date every man you see. I'm only saying that if you see a man out there, somewhere, who looks interesting to you, you should have the tools to take it to the next level (a date). By getting a date, you get the opportunity to see if you want to take it to an even higher level with that guy.

Master Dating is about being able to meet men who are outside of your circle. By using the techniques in this book, you should soon be able to meet men anywhere, and get the dates you want.

Change Is Good

There was a time when our survival as women, and as a species, was tied to having a mate. Women needed men to go out and kill dinner, and to provide shelter. Men needed women to have the babies and care for them. Neither could survive without the other.

Then we entered the Industrial Age and that changed everything. Survival became easier than it had been before. However, being unmarried past a certain age, or being a divorcee, carried with it a horrible stigma. So we all did our best to make sure that we didn't end up in either of those categories. People got married, and stayed married, even if they hated each other, in order to avoid that stigma.

Then came the Sixties, and with it the sexual revolution, equal rights and so forth. Getting divorced became the "in thing." Women were burning their bras, fighting for equal pay and making their presence and power known. All of our roles were changing, but into what?

Since then, we have come a long way. We have been forging new ground. Just like the Pilgrims, we did not know exactly where we were going, only that there must be something better than the way it was.

So where have we ended up? I would say on the independence and career front, we have done amazingly well—though there is still room to grow and trails to be blazed.

On the romantic front, however, we are faced with all new challenges. At least we do not feel a survival or social need to stay in a situation that may be toxic to us. I always hear people talk about "the old days." They will say, "There was a time when folks stayed together, 'till death did they part'." Yeah, but many of those people were totally miserable. They simply had no other choice.

Personally, I prefer today's challenges. I believe that we can find a healthy balance, one where people stay together not because they have to, but because they want to. We can find relationships that are right for us, not just "better than ending up an old maid." Then working things out in a relationship not only becomes possible but actually makes the most sense.

How "To Be or Not to Be"

Here is the difficulty that we now face. In the past, though things were not fair, they were clear. Women and men each had their roles. Men opened the door and brought home the bacon. Women cooked it up and then did the dishes (in bare feet). Now we don't have such clear-cut roles. This is better than it was, but we don't really know what to do or how to be.

This book is intended to help us all get beyond this confusion—not by divvying out new roles, or *"Rules,"* but by respecting each individual. (*The Rules* is a horribly popular book that tells women they must trick men into marrying them by pretending to be different than how they really are.)

Master Dating takes a completely different approach. We will concentrate on undoing old mindsets that do not work in our favor. We will also gain clarity about what is holding us back from having what we truly want. We learn to love, like and accept ourselves. We begin to see our value and learn how to be sure that men see it too. We will remove the barriers and overcome the obstacles that keep us from attaining the love life we desire.

Understanding the opposite sex's dilemma is an important part of getting to a place of hope, freedom and ease. By gaining compassion for what is most likely preventing a man from doing his part (asking you out), we are able to remove the blocks that stand in his way.

Master Date Safely

Please always be safe when you Master Date. The advice given in this book will enable you to meet men anywhere and get the dates you want. That means you may end up dating a stranger. There are certain precautions you should take to keep yourself safe.

If you do not know someone very well, I strongly advise that you not give them any more information than your first name and *maybe* your telephone number. I recommend that you take their number and call them. I have been told that a telephone number is enough for a person (who knows how to do it) to find out where you live. Do not give them your business card because they will then know where you work.

Before you go on a date with a stranger, you should know the first and last name of the man you are going out with. You should also know where he works, his home telephone number and work telephone number. Call him at each number to make sure he is "for real."

When you set a date with a stranger, always meet him at a public location. Never get into the car of a person you do not know well. If, while on the date, the two of you decide to go to another location, go in your own separate cars.

If you are concerned that by taking these precautions, a man will think you are paranoid and then not want to date you, you shouldn't be. Any man who disrespects your concern for your own safety is not a quality man, so you don't want to date him anyway. *Quality men do not disrespect women's feelings.*

I will tell a man, "It is my policy to go in separate cars and meet you in a public place." If he is a good man, he will understand and agree with—even encourage—any precautions I choose to take. He should logically and impersonally take into consideration that I do not know him yet. Openly taking these precautions actually serves as a way to learn whether you are talking to a man who has relationship potential or not. Consider this a natural test of the man's true nature.

Make a plan of what you will do on your date and stick to it. Tell a reliable friend or your mother everything you know about the guy. Also tell her where you are going and what you are going to do on your date. Then tell her when you will call to let her know you are home and safe. If you are not done having fun by the time you said you would call, call anyway. Tell her a new time and call again when you get home.

Be sure to read the Final Safety Warning at the back of this book.

Section I
Need to Know

PIP = Potentially Interesting Person

Chapter 1
Are You Level-Headed?

Love is like a video game. Just as you think you're getting the hang of it and finally get past that first level, you find out that the next level has all new challenges. No matter how good you get at any particular level, there is another level after that. This higher level will always initially stump you and quickly kill all of your little video men. Boom! GAME OVER.

Likewise with love, you can get very good at Level One, "Getting Dates," but you will then be faced with the next challenge of making a relationship work, and so on. You always end up "losing" your quarter, and if you want to play again you will have to be willing to "risk" another quarter. Since you cannot actually beat the video machine, the goal must be to enjoy playing as opposed to actually winning.

Even in a good and loving relationship there are difficulties, hurts and frustrations to overcome, and compromises to be made. In other words, no matter which way you slice it, romance is a challenge. Once you find that special someone, you enter the next level and the challenges simply change. Bottom line: In relationships you don't get to a point where you *never* feel some frustration, pain or insecurity; these feelings are part of romance on all levels.

Invest in Your Future

Marriage would be the equivalent of buying the home version of the video game. You may think that by having one at home you will never have to put in or "risk" another quarter, when in reality, you are just putting in all of your quarters up front.

The smart shopper does plenty of research so that she is aware of every option available to her before making her final decision. She tries out many different makes and models. She experiences a multitude of versions and options. She knows what features she likes and dislikes in a video game (or man). She has become clear after plenty of experience as to which positive traits she is (or is not) willing to give up in order to avoid which negative traits.

She only makes a commitment (buys one/marries one) when she feels sure she has found a model that she will not grow tired of. She is also sure that she has not picked one she will never be able to figure out. Instead she has found the model that will offer her a healthy challenge for the rest of her life. She is clear that she is committing to a "quality" machine, one that will not constantly break down, causing her endless frustration and grief. Or even worse than that, the darn thing can't be fixed and eventually just has to be trashed.

Do You Prefer the Frying Pan or the Fire?

Many relationships fail because the people in them got involved primarily so that they wouldn't have to remain miserably stuck in Level One—being single—any longer. Many singles have a false belief that if they were not single, life would be perfect.

This book is not only about mastering Level One, "Getting Dates." It's about truly enjoying being single. Desperation can lead us to make bad choices for ourselves. I believe that it is always better to strive to move towards something wonderful than to be running like hell from something awful—also known as the best way to get from the frying pan into the fire.

A dear and brilliant friend of mine, Chelsea, has a great analogy for this. She says, "Think of it this way: If you are running away from something (literally), where should you be looking? Behind you, at the thing you are trying to get away from, so you can keep an eye on how much distance there is between you and it? No! If you did, you would be very likely to trip over or run into the things in your path. Ouch! That is neither fun nor effective."

Chelsea says, "It would be much wiser to first decide where you want to end up; then keep your eye on it and head straight for it. This way, you are looking in front of you as you run. Then you can see and avoid the things that will trip you up and/or clunk you in the head, which would only cause you pain and slow you down!!"

Read the Instructions First

This book is intended to serve as a manual for mastering Level One of this complicated game called romance. There is a misconception in love and video games that the first level is the easiest level to master, when actually it is the most difficult.

Yes, once we have mastered Level One, the higher levels appear to be more difficult. Note, however, that it takes less time and

DOUBT
LOW ESTEE
FEAR
ACFernandez

effort to get to Level Three from Level Two, than it took to get past Level One. This is because when we first try to play a particular game, we don't even know what our goal is, let alone the strategy—not to mention what button does what.

It seems that in the romance game we have overlooked the difficulties of Level One and are already trying to master Level Two and so on. There are many great books written about how to make a relationship work. This book is not one of them. In this book, we will only be dealing with the mastery and enjoyment of Level One.

My hope is to cut down immensely on the frustrations associated with getting the dates you want, while leading you to great and fun "wins." This book will explain in detail how to overcome the obstacles, avoid potential pitfalls, and always score the bonus points. Before you know it, you will be getting all the dates you want, with the quality men you want, and truly RELISHING being single.

Chapter 2
Beauty Schmeauty

For those of you who may feel a bit insecure about your appearance, I want to reassure you. While I am by no means dog meat, many of the women who are amazed by my ability to meet and attract quality men are far prettier than I. And I am not being humble.

Never Let Your Opinions About Your Looks Stand in Your Way

The guy you are interested in may have a completely different taste in women's looks than you have. You may think that women who look like wafers (waifs) are the most attractive. He may think that Marilyn Monroe was God's gift. According to today's measuring stick for weight, Marilyn Monroe would be at Weight Watchers with a low self-image.

It's all about where you come from in dealing with the opposite sex. What I see happening so much is that when women don't think of themselves as beautiful, they project their opinion onto men in general. Women then give up, and don't put themselves out there. This may make men see these women as "difficult to approach." If you think you may fall into that category, don't worry. We've got this covered later in the book.

Positive Proof

Getting dates and attracting quality men has nothing to do with beauty. I promise you that. I can even prove it to you. It's easy. Average people are not beautiful by definition. Right? They are average. You and I are our own worst critics and I will take no argument on that one. So if you consider yourself to be average, you're really at the very least a bit above.

If you consider yourself below average, then you are probably *at least* average. The average person gets married approximately 1.6 times. This proves that looks don't really stand in the way of romance.

What if you think you are outright unattractive? There are tons of happily married "unattractive" people out there! I put "unattractive" in quotation marks because it is subjective. One of the qualities of the quality man we are looking for is that *he* can see *our* beauty.

I know so many women who society would deem unattractive, yet who are in great relationships that I aspire to, and with incredibly wonderful men (and I bet you do too)! This quality man sees the beauty of the woman he loves, even if you or I, or even society, would overlook it. I also know many gorgeous women who can't seem to get a date. If you fall into that category, don't worry. We will cover your dilemma later in the chapter "Open Sesame."

Chapter 3
Monkey Business

I view being single as one big research project. I have found that some men have a negative reaction to this outlook. I think it's because they simply misunderstand my position.

One man told me it made him feel like he was a monkey in a cage, and I was the scientist messing with his mind to find out what happens. Although that does sound like fun (hmmm…), I assure you that in this equation I am just as much a monkey as he is. To me, it's all about self-discovery.

I have become quite clear that when it comes to romance, I have yet to even understand my own mind's inner workings. The best way I can figure to learn the answers to the quandaries I have in my relationship to men is to submerge myself in the questions while trying out different answers, methods, and, well…men.

Odd-Shaped Peg

Finding "The One" is like a numbers game. Here is my "Peg/Hole Philosophy" in a nutshell. We all know it is futile to try to put a square peg into a round hole. I say, in relationships we are all either pegs or holes. We are out there trying to find the peg or hole that fits nicely with ours.

I am an odd-shaped peg. I am not normal in many ways. This is not good or bad. It just means that I am looking for an odd-shaped hole, one that fits comfortably with me. The odder (more unique) you are, the higher the numbers in the numbers game. (Please always remember that the right man for you will love you most for what is most unique about you.)

Even if you are fairly "normal," you are probably still looking for a one-in-a-hundred guy. As odd as I am, it's probably one in a thousand. So let's say the average is one in five-hundred. If that's you, you may have to date a lot of guys to find "The One." Of course, he could be number 12!

So Many Men, So Little Faith

Believe me, it *is* really true that there are literally hundreds of thousands of wonderful and upstanding single men out there thinking, "I wish I had a girlfriend. I wish I had a date for this Saturday night!" And there are hundreds of thousands of great single women out there thinking the exact same thing. Every day these men and women pass each other by in the street, the store, the elevator, never realizing that the person they just passed could have been that "date for Saturday night"!

This missed realization is one of the first and biggest obstacles between you and the love life you desire. Once you come to this realization, a never-ending hallway of doors becomes visible to you. This book is intended to be the "master key" to those doors—or at least a good lock-pick set.

Of Needles and Haystacks

If you begin to feel discouraged, I want you to hold on to these two concepts: One, everyone always says it is horribly difficult, if not impossible, to find a needle in a haystack. However, sometimes you sit yourself right down in the middle of a big pile of hay and "OUCH!" Guess what, you found it. It *can* be that easy.

Two, Confucius say: "Don't be so impatient. Everything worth finding is worth searching for."

For instance, think about how many women you have met in your entire life. Probably thousands, right? And of those thousands, how many have you decided to make your close personal friend? Most likely just a handful.

Now think about this: We hold a significant other to a much higher standard than we hold a friend to. This is not unfair, it is logical. For instance, you can be friends with someone even if their style of raising children or handling money conflicts with our own. Those factors in a friend will not have an impact on your life. But if you marry a man who you conflict with in these ways, it will definitely affect your life, and in a big way.

The point I am trying to make is, we tend to think that "The One" should just come to us, that finding him should not take time and searching. But statistically speaking, most people are not "our people." This is proven by how many people we have *not* turned into our close personal friends.

We can have many friends, so no *one* of them has to fulfill all the many aspects of what we are looking for. But, since we can really only have one significant other, we must scrutinize a potential mate much more than a potential friend.

We all basically accept that finding a close friend is a rare and special thing. However, when we look back on how we became friends with that person, it was probably no more difficult than sitting on a needle in a haystack. Though it most likely felt better.

I am not saying that "The One" will not be magically dropped into our lap—I am totally open to that. I am just saying it is possible that finding "Mr. Right" will take time and research. This is not a bad thing once you learn to enjoy the process.

A large part of the research is understanding and mastering our own selves, and learning to recognize "The One" when we see him. This can be a wondrous and magical journey if we remain patient and open to our own self-discovery. In search of yourself, I highly recommend reading anything written by the author SARK. My personal favorite is *Succulent Wild Woman.*

Chapter 4
Who Am I to Say?

I am a 33-year-old hairdresser. I own and operate a funky little shop in Los Angeles called *The Jungle*. I have been doing hair, in business for myself, for 13 years. I love my work, and my clients, and feel lucky to have found my niche early in life.

I am not a psychologist or a therapist. I am a real person out there on the front lines, just like you. My credentials are that my advice has been proven over and over to work for the many women who seek it out and use it. I like to joke that I am a certified L.O.P. (Life Observer/Participant). When I grow up, I would like to become a philosopher.

You will notice that this book is written in a very conversational style. I am not trying to fool anyone, I am not an academic. I am a hairdresser. As the movie cops say, "It's not just a job, it's who I am." Believe me, I have heard it all standing behind that chair, and I have been paying attention. What you read in this book is real life!

Compiling Data

My profession has put me in a unique position for getting an incredible amount of research material on the subject of romance. I have heard it said that the only person who knows more about your personal life than your therapist is your hairdresser. At least at my shop, I believe that to be true.

I have to thank all of my clients, both male and female. Without them sharing their experiences and frustrations, what worked for them and what did not, I would never have "mastered" this whole "dating thing." Much of my research was done by inadvertently interviewing my hair clients.

The rest of my research was also unintentional. My ex-husband had tons of male friends. During our marriage, they seemed to think of me as one of the guys, but with the inside scoop on women. My husband and I had separate telephone lines, and sometimes it seemed as though his friends called me more often than him.

They were always calling to get my advice on some "girl situation." They would say "You have to tell me how to proceed." Consequently, I was getting an in-depth education on what men go through when dealing with the opposite sex. I got an incredibly clear understanding of what men think, and what holds them back in the romance department.

To Have or to Be Had: That Is the Question

Even in these modern days, women are "had" by the notion that we are supposed to just sit passively by and wait for a man to ask us out. I am not saying that having the man do the asking is bad; in fact, I prefer it.

What I am saying is that as a modern woman I am not good at sitting passively and waiting for anything. I feel I need to be proactive in all areas of my life. As women, we have many options available to us to have a say and an impact on whether or not we get a date.

I have learned a great method to lower the walls that stand between ourselves and any relationship we want to create. The trick is simply this: understand the dilemmas the other person faces. This works with men and everyone else.

For instance, if you're going for a job interview, it is wise to get into the head of the interviewer. What are her (or his) hopes and fears? When you can see the other person's barriers, you can move them out of the way with ease. The same holds true with men. They are really just afraid of the same things you and I are, but from a different point of view.

Understanding men's point of view very well has probably done more towards making me the official Master Dater than anything else. That and the fact that I have been out there doing plenty of field research, putting my hypotheses to the test.

We *can* empower men who are interested in us to ask us out. Once you get the idea, it's not even hard to do. Especially if you do the two very special exercises I prescribe later in this book, you will find that your part comes easily and naturally.

Who, Me?

It all started many years ago, long before I ever even thought of writing a book. Over the years, I have given tons of dating advice. Clients would call at all hours of the day and night seeking my advice. They would say, "I'm not really ready for a haircut yet, but I was hoping you could help me figure out what to do about this guy situation I've got going." A few times women in my chair have admitted, "I wasn't really all *that* due for a cut, but I had to consult with you about this guy I like."

I have successfully advised women of all ages, ranging from 12 to 83. These women come from extremely varied backgrounds. Some of them are at the top of their profession, while others are just starting out. Some are heads of corporations and have earnings well into the six figures. Some of these women are stunningly beautiful, while others are not so "well endowed."

The funny thing is that when it comes to romance, we are all in the same boat and have the same issues. We all feel the same butterflies in our stomachs when we're "one on one" with a guy we have the "hots" for. We are all held back by the same fears, no matter what category we may fall into. Loneliness is also universal. And so are the techniques that are effective to attract men, start conversations with them and empower them to ask us out.

When I became single again after my marriage ended, I started putting my own advice into action, along with the research that I had unwittingly been accumulating. With shocking success, I began to meet and attract quality men.

I am often asked how I decided to write this book. If three people tell me (in unrelated circumstances) to do the same thing, I take it as a sign, so I do it. In this situation, more than ten people emphatically convinced me to write this book. So here it is. I hope that it will be helpful and effective for all who take the time to read it.

When I began writing the book, many people started asking about seminars. So I also began speaking publicly. Those seminars were incredible for me in so many ways, but mostly for these two reasons: One, because it was massively satisfying to see that I could make a positive difference in the lives of many women at once. And two, because I really got down to the nitty-gritty of the problems women face in hooking up with the opposite sex. I would say the most powerful realization for me was that no matter how different the women were, their issues were the same.

Damned If I Do, Damned If I Don't

People often feel that they need to know about my romantic status. I'm going to cover that here and now, because it enables me to make a very important point. Before I tell you, I want to say that it's sort of a "damned if I do, damned if I don't" situation.

If I'm in a relationship, then you may think, "What does she know about it? She's not out here on the front lines!" If I'm single, you may think, "If she's so good at meeting quality men and getting the dates she wants, then why is she still single?"

Having said that, I'll tell you that during the evolution of this book (a little more than a year and a half) I have had two committed relationships. One lasted three months and the other one nine months. As I am writing this, I am single and dating. I am really enjoying the total control of my remote control. Both boyfriends were absolutely wonderful quality men, as are most of the men I date. However, they were not the right fit for me.

Feelin' Groovy

The important thing to note here is that I am happy and really loving my life as it is. Because I am enjoying being single and feel content with that status, I feel no push to try to force a relationship. I also know that as soon as I decide that I would like to be in a relationship again, one will be right around the corner. I know this because I know myself well. I am clear that I am the type of woman that quality men are looking for. (Soon, *you* will also know this about yourself.)

My wish for all women is that before they get to "The One," they come to a place where they are totally happy being single. So happy, in fact, that the only reason they would be willing to give up singlehood is that they've found something *even* better. For instance, an incredibly supportive, nurturing, compatible, passionate partner would (probably) qualify as something better. This happy-enough-being-single-to-wait-for-a-great-relationship state of mind is achieved when we complete ourselves independently. This state of mind is also the healthiest possible place from which to start a relationship.

This is what you have to do...

Chapter 5
Hot Air

Giving advice is like breaking wind. They are both just air in motion making a noise. And sometimes they stink! That's the value of other people's opinions about how you should live your life whether it's my advice or anyone else's. It is always healthy to be open to advice, but only actually *do* what feels right for you.

You Are like a Snowflake

You are a totally unique individual. In this book, I will be describing many possible scenarios. I want to make myself perfectly clear right off that I am not talking about *"Rules"* in this book. When it comes to interpersonal relationships, there are no pre-described answers that are right for everyone. One size never fits all! The individual must always be taken into consideration. And I know that you are capable of thinking for yourself.

In this book you will find some theories that are based on generalities. I'm not saying that all of the people in a particular group are one way or another. If you don't see yourself in something I have said, then it may not relate to you.

This Book Is like a Shoe

You know the old saying "If the shoe fits, wear it." This book is designed to offer you a place to stand, or to come from. It's about a new outlook and a different perspective. Try these philosophies on and see if they fit. If my ways fit you perfectly, you can use them literally, though that's not necessarily what I am suggesting.

There is no way I can write a script for you that will fit every situation, nor would I want to. I want you to be creative. Come up with your own stance so that you can work with each situation as it unfolds. If the shoe doesn't fit or is not right for you, discard it or alter it accordingly. Or find yourself a pair that fit you perfectly.

This book will be most effective for you if as you read it you look at where I'm coming from rather than the words I am using. Then you will be able to develop your own Master Dating techniques that fit your individual style and personality and feel comfortable for you.

I never believe my way is the "right way" or the only way. I am sharing with you what works for me and has worked for many who have taken my advice. If you like it, and it works for you, keep it and share it with a friend. If not, keep on being the open-minded person that you are and keep trying on new ideas. Eventually you will find the perfect fit for you. Best of luck!

Chew on This

My wise old grandfather insisted that I include the following advice in this book. He said that many people will read a self-help book like this one from a perspective that cheats them out of the benefit. He says that people are tempted to just sit back and check off each tidbit of information. They decide "Yes, I agree with that" or "No, I don't agree with that."

Grandpa says that this is not being open and never leads to learning anything new, since you "already know what you already know." He says in order to learn from any philosophy we must bite off the entire concept, then chew on it for a while. Then we can decide if we want to spit it out or swallow and be fortified by it.

I chewed on what my grandfather said for a while, and I decided he had a point. It made me think of something a guy once said to me: "Here's the problem I have with women in business. They can be totally reasonable rational beings. Then once every 28 days, they become 'had' by their hormones and become completely irrational and unreasonable for a few days. Men are much easier for me to deal with because they are predictable. Men are *always* 'had' by their hormones. They are always unreasonable and irrational. So I always know what to expect and can take action accordingly."

When this guy started his statement, I was ready to go through the roof. However, when I heard all of what he had to say, I realized that his statement was not all bad or all wrong. I even felt some compassion for how it was for him.

Actually what this man said made a difference for me. In the past I would often tell the women in my life when it was "*that* time of the month," so they would know what to expect. Now I also find a way to let the men in my life know when they may be walking into a mine-field, in advance of my "going ballistic."

Section II
How to Get from Hmmm?…TO HIM!!

Chapter 6
Step One, I Contact!

Usually the first contact made with a "Potentially Interesting Person" (from this point forward they will be referred to as "PIPs") is eye contact. There are a few different types of eye contact.

There is the "Across the Room" eye contact, the "In Passing" eye contact (when a PIP is passing by you) and the all-important "Conversational" eye contact. Each is different in many respects, but similar in that they are all ways of sneaking in communication without words. In order for that contact to have the desired impact, it must be delivered well. It is fun and easy when you know how. Perfecting this ability will be incredibly useful for you in meeting and attracting quality men!

"Across the Room"

So you're at the 7-Eleven, a restaurant or club, the market or any public place, when you see a PIP. How do you get from hmmm?...TO HIM! Often in these situations, you'll want to make eye contact before a conversation begins.

When making this kind of eye contact, remember that you are trying to convey a message with your eyes. People have told me that they are no good at eye-contact flirting because they always end up looking away—when really, this action is in fact conveying the desired message. Think about it. If a man stares at you and when you look back at him he doesn't end up looking away, you feel uncomfortable and intimidated—more like you're being *stalked* than flirted with! A man will also feel uncomfortable if a woman overstays her gaze.

The ideal "Across the Room" eye-contact flirt only makes contact for two or three seconds, and then shyly, must turn away. Usually this will make you smile, which is again a perfect communication—friendly and pleasant. It shows you're happy that he looked back and showed interest in you. Even blushing works in your favor, so don't try to hide it. In these ways, you are using your nervous energy to your advantage.

It's important that you let him catch you looking back at him. Subconsciously, this tells him you are interested. If he doesn't catch you looking back at him, he may decide you are not interested. Then he may not be able to get up the nerve to come over and start a conversation with you. Side note: If he's looking at you when you look back at him, that's a pretty good sign he is interested in you. If he isn't looking at you, that's not necessarily a sign that he's not interested in you.

In a situation where you have the time, this entire sequence of looking, looking away and looking back, should repeat itself a few times before you move forward. This kind of eye-contact flirting is most effective in a restaurant, club, or in line at an amusement park or the DMV. Use it in any situation where you and the PIP are going to be in the same place for a while.

"In Passing"

If a PIP is walking past you, you must think quickly. You must deliver a powerful enough, *instant*, high-impact eye contact to warrant him coming back for more. A deliberate and direct "pupil to pupil" contact is necessary! If you can think fast enough, say "Hi" and/or "How are you?" Either way you absolutely must SMILE! This step is VERY IMPORTANT!!

If you are able to deliver a direct enough hit, the PIP may come up with some excuse to come back and start a conversation with you. Again, allow him to catch you looking back at him. If he's not looking back, keep watching him so that if he does look back at you, he will see you looking at him. If and when he does look back at you, show that you are happy with a huge, kind of shy, smile. This is the only way he will be able to get up the nerve to come back and talk to you. It is also a good idea to try to find a reason of your own to pass him again

This method can be challenging. Even if you think fast enough and get up the nerve, it may not work, though often enough it does. My clients and I have shared many success stories about using this method. Think of it this way. If you try and fail, you have lost nothing. If you don't try, you will almost definitely lose the opportunity to meet the guy. We must be very direct in this situation because it takes an incredible amount of nerve for the guy to do his part. Therefore, we must *really* do our part.

"Conversational"

When you have the opportunity to "conversate" with a PIP, use it to your FULL advantage. You may not get a second chance. The trick is, when you look at him, look him straight in the eye.

Make an even stronger impact by focusing directly on his pupils. You are almost searching for the inner anatomy of his eyeball as you speak and listen. You must hold this contact for a little bit longer than is comfortable in order to get the desired result. Finally, you must let go of his optic nerve. You may notice him trying to get your "tractor beam" back onto him. This is a very good sign that he *is* interested.

For the man on the receiving end of this communication, it is a clear sign of interest in him not just as a date—but as an individual. You are giving him all of your attention. He is highly complimented and feels deeply respected. If a guy is interested in you, this will go a long way in empowering him to ask you out. We will go into more powerful ways to help/get him to ask you out throughout the rest of the book.

Incidentally, by looking this closely at people, you also get a great read on exactly who they really are. Many times they will reveal to you things about themselves that they ordinarily would not. They will say, " I don't know why I am telling you all of this. I usually don't tell such details about my life to a virtual stranger."

If a man cannot return your gaze, it may be a sign that he is hiding something. It could also be extreme shyness or intimidation, but when shyness or intimidation is the problem, he will usually try to reconnect with you once you look away. Many of the women I have taught this method to have agreed with me. "It's almost as though I can read his mind and see through any facade when I look at a person this closely."

By using this method, I have found that I can get a sense of a person's nature. Sometimes I see kindness or power. Occasionally, I have gotten a very bad vibe or gut instinct. The times I have ignored that feeling, I was sorry. It's important that you use this technique not only as a way of impacting a PIP, but as a way to start figuring out if this person is right for you.

Chapter 7
Tennis, Anyone?

So you've got the eye-contact thing down pat. What do you do after that? And what do you do when there is no time for making even the "in passing" eye contact? Here are some ideas for dealing with situations when you only have a moment to strike.

Think Fast!

Let's say you see a PIP as you arrive at the elevator. He's going up and you're going down. Two strangers passing in the lobby. The elevator doors open. What to do? Think fast! No time for this eye-contact stuff, you've got only seconds to make your move. This calls for drastic measures!

If you think he might be interested in you, you could accidentally drop something. Say he quickly bends down to chivalrously retrieve it for you (the plot thickens). This could be a sign that he's interested in you. He wants to talk to you. He does not want to get on the elevator, but he needs your help! He needs a reason to stay!

You look him directly in the eye as you sincerely thank him, thinking, "How do I give this guy an excuse to miss his elevator?" You could "accidentally" dump the entire contents of your purse onto the floor, "Oops!" If he misses the elevator to help you, he is either a really nice guy, or he digs you, or both. GREAT!!

So there you stand, the guts of your purse sprawled out on the marble floor of some office building, and this "tall, dark and handsome" is down on his hands and knees...helping you pick them up. As a side note, if you are particularly fond of this method, take my advice, which is quite similar to your mom's advice about wearing clean underwear. You know, in case you get into a terrible accident...you don't want to get caught with embarrassing items in your purse. Tampons, your diaphragm, or vaginal itch cream are examples of things that may not exactly create the best impression!

1 2 3 4 5 6 7 8 9 10

Serve! With a Smile

Now you may be thinking, "Yeah, that's great, but what are the chances that it's going to happen in front of the elevator for me?" Slim?! What I want for you to take from this example is the concept of taking personal responsibility for meeting the guy. No more sitting on the sidelines watching the ball go back and forth, or even standing on the court waiting for a serve to come your way. Grab the ball and serve it! If he makes the slightest effort to hit the ball back to you, *don't wait*, serve another!

This example is just an illustration of one way to do that. Of course, the method of dropping something and allowing a gentleman to retrieve it for you is a good way of making initial contact with a man in many situations. We will go further into how to take it from there in the following chapters.

Hindsight Is 20/20

As you begin to Master Date, you may find that you get flubbed up in the moment and miss an opportunity to get a date with a PIP. When this happens, it is important that you don't allow yourself to feel bad about it, or in any way beat yourself up for it. If you start feeling bad, you will not want to go on trying, and you may quit.

More importantly, if you're mad at yourself, you won't want to think about what happened. Thinking about it, however, is a very important step. Go back in your mind to the situation. Now, when you aren't nervous, think of other ways that you could have handled the situation.

By doing so, you begin to generate your own techniques. The next time you are faced with a similar situation, you are more likely to remember your own technique than one of mine.

If at first, you don't succeed... Remember, in your early life there was a time when you couldn't find that hole in your face where the food goes in, but you kept trying. You may have made a mess but eventually you learned, and now you can feed yourself. Dating is a skill and, as with everything else in life, the more you do it the better you get at it. The point I am trying to make is, it is better to open your mouth and miss (say something stupid) a few times than to never learn to eat (get a date)!

Chapter 8
Smooth Starts

Why is it so difficult to start a conversation with a stranger? It's just two people exchanging words. This *seems* as natural as responding "gesundheit!" to a sneeze.

I think there are two basic stumbling blocks that account for the bulk of what stops us from talking to strangers. One: figuring out what to say on the spur of the moment. Two: *nerves!* The next few chapters are dedicated to handling the first one. Rest assured that the rest this book is laced with great stuff that will not only calm, but actually strengthen your nerves. By the time you are finished reading it you will have nerves of (stainless) steel.

Talk Talk Talk

First and most important, OPEN YOUR MOUTH!! Say something! SAY ANYTHING! If you can think fast enough, try to make it something that could segue into more of a conversation. Try to lead into a conversation about a hobby or work, either yours or his.

Bring up something that he could ask you about, or something that you can ask him about. If all else fails, joke around while you try to think of something. I find that I get a little clumsy due to nervousness in these situations. So it's easy to joke about myself. If you find you also get a bit clumsy, know that most men find this trait to be endearing in this kind of situation. In other words, early klutz-dom is cute!

The Question Is the Answer

Asking questions works better than making a statement because the guy has to answer you. If you just make a statement, the PIP may be interested in you, but not be able to think fast enough to come up with something else to say. So help him out.

Keeping the conversation going by asking questions also gives him a moment to figure out that he may be talking to that date for Saturday night he was hoping to run into. Plus, in the time it takes for him to answer you, you get a moment to think about where you can take the conversation next.

A good way to begin in many situations is, "Do you know the closest place to get a cup of java, or a bite to nibble?" There are two reasons why this is so good. If he *is* interested in you, he now knows where you're going to be for the next twenty minutes. So if it dawns on him that you could be that "date for Saturday night," he can just happen to show up at the place he told you about. Then the two of you will have another chance to "get it together."

Better yet, if he knows where the place is (assuming he has caught your drift), he could offer to show you the way. If he does not offer, I would ask him, very politely (with a coy inviting smile), "Would you possibly be willing to show me? You see, I'm directionally challenged and get easily turned around." If he does show you, you're ninety-percent sure he is interested. Now you have the time it takes to get from here to there to open up the next opportunity and keep the interaction going.

Got Guts?

If you are a gutsy gal or if you realize that you will not get another opportunity to meet a particular guy, you could try the following. If he doesn't offer to show you the way, you say with a warm smile, "Wait, that was the part where you were supposed to say, 'How about if I show you where it is and then join you?'" Though this is a bit forward, if the guy takes you up on your request that he ask to join you, he still considers that *he* asked *you.*

Anytime you are in a place where you "might" get a little lost, or not know how to find your intended destination, you could ask a fellow for help in the same way as above. Keep in mind that good (quality) men enjoy helping people.

The Inquisition

Here is another example of how to start and then keep the "convo" going. Compliment him. "Love that tie! (shirt, haircut, etc.) Hey, would you mind telling me where you got it?"..."Is that shop in the mall?"..."Do you know which local mall has that store?"..."Oh, do you know how I get to that mall from here?"..."Hmm, do you know how I would get there from the area where I work?"..."You do? Gee, you know the area well."...Or, if he doesn't know, "I've lived here X years and I still get lost!" Either way, "How long have you lived here?"..."Really, where are you from?"..."Oh, what's it like there as compared to here?"..."Very interesting, what made you decide to move here?"..."Wow, that's even more interesting. Tell me more."...(You get the point!)

If you're thinking, "I would never be that bold, it just isn't me," stop and think. If you are not a bold person, you are probably not looking for the pushy type of guy. Right? So how do two shy people get together? Someone is going to have to push past "the way they are" to make something happen.

Obviously, you only continue the inquisition if he's a willing participant. If the guy does not seem like he is enjoying the conversation, or if he seems to want to escape, let him. As soon as you get home, read the chapter "What If He Still Does Not Ask (or, How to Deal with Rejection)."

The trick is, if the guy seems even slightly interested, *you* personally keep the conversation going. Oftentimes the most wonderful men are the least slick around women. So don't hesitate to take the initiative, and keep taking it. You have nothing to lose by trying.

Strange Animals

The human animal has many strange and quirky traits. One of the oddest is that we (men and women) usually feel extremely uncomfortable with the idea of other people knowing that we like them. I feel it, too. But why? It really doesn't work in our favor.

Maybe it's the whole "avoiding risk" thing. If we never show that we like someone and then nothing comes of it, it feels less like rejection. Of course, we are also much less likely to end up with a date that way. If we don't show that we like a guy because we are afraid, and he doesn't show it because he is afraid, how the heck are we ever going to get together?

In some situations there is more time for beating around bushes than in others. If you work with a PIP, or he is part of your circle of friends, for example, you will probably be seeing more of each other. In these situations, it may be wise to take your time "letting the cat out of the bag." This way, you can avoid any uncomfortable feelings, should your affections not be returned. Keep in mind, however, that one of you will eventually have to take that risk.

Like Shooting Dead Fish in a Barrel

There are those that would advise you to act aloof in order to entice a man. They will say, "Men like women who are hard to get." This is true of some men, but I warn you that there are hazards involved in dating that type. They are unhealthy prospects, though they are a cinch to catch (all you have to do is *not* want them). It is nearly impossible to have a healthy relationship with these men because the moment you like them back and show it, it's "bye-bye," since you are now no longer "hard to get." It's kind of a Catch-22.

Healthy "quality men" like it when you like them. In fact, in survey studies, men in happy long-term relationships were asked, "What was the first thing that piqued your interest in your significant other?" A high percentage of the time the response was, "I could tell that she liked me."

I will add my own experience to that. In the past, there have been instances where I have liked a guy and been too shy to show it initially. Almost every time, as soon as I got up the nerve and showed that I was interested, he instantly became interested in me and shortly thereafter asked me out.

Interest Rating

I actually use showing a guy that I like him as kind of a test to see how emotionally healthy he is. If a lack of interest on my part interests him, then I'm not interested. If, however, he likes it that I like him, that makes me like him more. No matter how much I like a PIP, I will disqualify him if he is an unhealthy man who cannot handle being liked.

I am not recommending that you throw yourself at men, or push yourself on them. Usually when you push people in any direction, they will run the opposite way. The idea is to meet them at least halfway, and help make their job of meeting you easier by offsetting their fear of rejection.

The mental stance is like this: "I like you, and if you like me, we should go out." Can you see how there is nothing pushy, desperate or aloof in that? You are just holding confidently still, neither running nor chasing. You are simply open to the PIP being interested in you, or not. Confidence is ALWAYS attractive.

Chapter 9
Whad-d'ya-know, Joe?

Another very effective method of starting a conversation and keeping it going is to find a subject that he's "in the know" about. Find something you could be interested in enough to ask him if he would be willing to sit down with you over coffee or lunch and explain it to you. By asking him to coffee or lunch, as opposed to dinner or a drink, you are reserving the *actual* "asking for a date" for him.

Mind you, I am not against asking men out. But personally, I just like it better when they do the asking. Relationships are most tenuous in the early stages. There are so many places where things can go awry when people are just starting to get to know each other. Most people (men and women) feel more comfortable with the traditional roles. You know, where the man clubs the woman over the head, and drags her off to his cave. So why complicate things by creating an unfamiliar dynamic? Especially when it is so easy to empower him to ask you out!

Shop Talk

Talking about his work is usually a good idea. As a side note, I have found some men to be sensitive if you ask too soon about their work. He may feel you are fishing to see how much money he makes. It is best to encourage him to bring up his profession.

One good way to do this is to mention your own work and then ask him about his. Here is an example of how to do that: I might say to any guy I'm standing next to anywhere, "Oh my feet are killing me! As a hairdresser it's a job hazard." He will usually then say something on the order of, "Long day, huh? I know what you mean." Then I can say, "Yes, do you work on your feet too?" His response is usually something like "Oh, me? I'm a botanist, I spend my days bent over a bunch of plants." BOOM, we're are in a conversation and I can ask him all sorts of questions about his "incredibly interesting" career.

Really, he could explain anything from the weather, to his opinion of the proposition on the next ballot, you name it! His profession usually makes it easy. For instance, say you find out he's a stockbroker. You could say something like, "A stockbroker, ya' don't say. I wonder if you wouldn't mind explaining to me whether mutual funds are really better than money markets, and why?"

If he's a telephone repairman, you could ask, "Can I call you to find out what it takes to be a telephone repair dude? See, I have a girlfriend who thinks she wants to be one. Do you think being a woman would stand in the way of doing that job?" Whatever he answers, you say, "Really, why?"

If he's a car radio installation manager, you could ask him, "Would you be willing to take a look at my car? Maybe you could help me to figure out what would be the best and most cost-effective car radio to get for my car? Do you think that Japanese-made electronics are better than American-made?" Again, don't forget to say, "Really, why?"

You get the idea. Just be open to each situation as it unfolds and go with the flow. Make him feel confident about asking you out on a date. Remember: To him, you are a stranger out of the blue who might get offended if he is too forward.

There are an endless number of possible scenarios, and within each scenario, there are many ways to get a "convo" started and keep it going. I will now give you some more scenarios and options. It's a good idea for you to make up one or two of your own for each situation. Also think up some scenarios on your own so that you know you're learning to generate your own ways of Master Dating, not just reading a fun book.

Penny for Your Thoughts

Say you're at the 7-Eleven, when you see a PIP. If you're near the sunglasses, you could ask him his opinion on which pair he likes best on you. You could start explaining that you recently lost your favorite pair. As things progress, you could keep the conversation rolling with, "I go back and forth in my mind about whether or not it makes sense to invest in a nice pair of expensive sunglasses or not. What do you think?"... "Where do you buy your sunglasses?"... (Then you can go back into the inquisition from the chapter "Smooth Starts.")

Or if you're there getting a soda, you could ask him to show you how the soda fountain works. You could explain "I usually never drink soda, but today I need the sugar rush! Is it self-serve or what?"..."Do you know which kind has the most caffeine?"..."Where do they keep the lids?"..."Do you think diet soda really makes you lose weight?"... "Isn't it funny when you see someone buy diet soda and Twinkies at the same time?"...

Maybe you're at the gas station when you spot a friendly-looking target. You could ask him to explain what he knows about the difference between supreme and super-supreme gas. You can help the conversation to continue by asking him, "Do you really recommend one over the other?"..."Which one?"..."Why?"...

If you're at the market in the produce section, you could ask, "Do you know how to pick a ripe persimmon?"...'How do you think they came up with the name persimmon anyway?"..."I mean, I can understand how oranges got their name, I can understand how the watermelon got its name, but how do you think the persimmon got its name?"...

What if you are nowhere near the produce department? You could ask him for other help. For instance, you could say, "If you were bacon bits where would you be?"..."With the salad fixin's or canned meat?"..."Who do you think makes the decision on these things anyway?"..."Do you think they have a committee of 'power-hungry, suit-wearing' egomaniacs who debate these issues in sky-scraping board rooms for a living, or what?"...

Need a Hero?

The point is, not only do you take responsibility for starting the conversation, you've also got to keep it going. Questions that lead to questions are the ticket. Questions that he can expound upon and that make it easy for him to flirt with you work best. Good men love to help, quality men enjoy being your hero!

Remember, find a way to ask a man to help you. In many situations you can ask a PIP to reach something for you or hand something to you. Say you're at the market in the cereal aisle. You could ask him, "Have you seen the Cap'n Crunch's with the Crunch Berries?" Think of any way to request a PIP's assistance.

If any man ever snubs you or is less than happy to help, this tells you a lot about his character. You get to find out real quick that you wouldn't even want to date him. Make sure that he is actually giving you a bad attitude and not just feeling shy. I do this by saying something like, "Don't mind me, I'm just friendly." Note: This is not an apology!

I like this approach because if he is interested in me, my comment makes it easy for him to let me know. I have even gotten into conversations with men about how being friendly used to be normal. If the guy is not interested in me, my statement makes my talking to him less of a flirtation. There's nothing wrong with saving a little face, once you find out that the man is not interested.

Watch closely for any sign that a PIP might be interested in you. Unless he shows you that he DEFINITELY IS NOT interested, assume that he is. Assume that the guy just does not know how to proceed. Many wonderful men are quite humble and therefore a bit dense when it comes to realizing that a woman is flirting with them. If he does shut you down, *assume that he is either married or gay.* There now, doesn't that feel better?

Chapter 10
Trick?... or Treat!!

By far none, my favorite way to open a conversation with a PIP is the oldest trick in the book. It's the old "Don't I know you from somewhere?" line. But I don't say it exactly that way because it doesn't require enough of a detailed answer from the man. I say, "Gosh, you look familiar to me. Do I look at all familiar to you?"

So Many Pro's, No Con's

Oh, there are so many wonderful things about the "You look familiar" approach! Where do I begin? First off, it starts a conversation that can go on as long as both people want it to. They may have to kick you out of the establishment you're at when it's time to close, if the two of you still haven't figured out where you know each other from. That's all right. You can always continue the investigation over dinner.

This approach also gives you the opportunity to find out an incredible amount of information about a PIP's life, and without ever appearing to be fishing. If he is interested in you, he may respond with "Maybe" or, even better, "Yeah, you do look familiar." Then you start in with "Where could I know you from? Hmmm...Where did you go to kindergarten?" (Okay, that may be pushing it.) "Where did you go to school?" ..."Where did you grow up?"..."Where have you worked?"..."What kinds of hobbies or groups are you into?"..."Could I have met you at Temple Beth Shalom?"...

See how you inadvertently get oodles of info about him and his life? And you're just trying to figure out where you might know him from. Likewise, he gets to find out a lot about you! If things are going well, this gives you the opportunity to bring it to the next level.

Very Inviting

For instance, in figuring out where the two of you might know each other from, he might say that you may have seen him roller-blading at Venice Beach. He tells you that he goes there all the time. Then you could say, "Oh, you roller-blade? I've always wanted to try roller-blading. If I only had someone to go with!"

He might say, "Do you ballroom dance? We may have seen each other at the place where I teach ballroom dance lessons? Or maybe it was at one of the places where I go dancing?" This gives you the opportunity to say, "I have always thought I would be good at ballroom dancing, if I had a good partner to teach me."

He might say something like, "Do you ever go to the bar called 'The Football Freak'?" Then (*only if he is really cute*) you could say, "Oh, you're a football fanatic. I have always thought I would enjoy 'spectating' that sport. If I only had someone who would really explain it to me!"

I think you get the idea. You get the opportunity to practically invite him to ask you out on a date. If he *is* interested in you, he *will* ask you out! Tip: When you are saying the part that is "inviting," you want to look him very deep in the eye with a big smile. As always, after making the direct eye contact, looking away and/or blushing is just fine.

Party Hardy

Another great aspect of this method is that you get to find out very quickly whether or not the party of the first part (HIM) is interested in partying with the party of the second part (YOU). If he is not interested, you'll get a quick glance followed by a "No, I don't think I know you." Before you get upset, and start feeling all rejected, dejected, *brung* down, hung down and strung out, WAIT! I will cover that in the chapter "What If He Still Does Not Ask (or, How to Deal with Rejection)."

If he responds with a "Maybe," he might be interested. But if he responds with "What hospital were you born in?" YOU'RE IN LIKE FLYNN! So, with this method, you get a good reading on how interested he is in you, all kinds of details on his life, and opportunities to invite him to invite you out. What more could you want in an approach?

This method may seem to be a bit "game-ish," dishonest or manipulative, and as you will soon know, I am against all of those. Allow me to explain my rationale. First off, if the guy has two nostrils, he looks like someone you have known! So in fact, the statement that he looks familiar is not actually dishonest.

Secondly, if the guy is interested in you, I assure you he is going to be so glad that you figured out some way to start a conversation and keep it going until he got up the nerve (with your help) to ask you out! If you don't believe me, or even if you do, try confessing your strategy (best to come clean) on the first date. See how he feels about it. I bet he'll be flattered by it, and thank you for it. This is a manipulation an interested party *will* appreciate.

Head Swelling

One final note on this method. If a PIP ever asks *you* this question, make sure that you don't actually "know him from somewhere," before you get too excited about him wanting to go out with you.

Once, in a department store, I went up to the counter to ask a question. The handsome gentleman there looked at me and said, "You look familiar, don't I know you from somewhere?" My ego had already begun swelling my head to at least twice its normal size when he said, "Oh, I know where I know you from, Tae Kwon Do class." I felt so embarrassed about what I had thought that I couldn't even continue flirting with him.

Section III
Philosophy Break

Chapter 11
Is It Really Worth All of This?

After everything you have just read you may be asking yourself, "Is my love life really worth all of this?" Of course, I cannot answer that question for you. However, I would like to pose another question to you that may help you decide exactly how much effort you are willing to put into your love life.

If You Choose Not to Decide, You Have Made Your Choice

I am going to present you with a choice. You can only choose one of the following options. The first option is that you can have the loving, supportive, nurturing relationship of your dreams—the perfect man for you and the perfect relationship in every way. True love that will last forever, exactly as you would have it. The second choice is a million dollars. Which would you choose?

I have asked this question to hundreds of people, and so far only one person has chosen the money. I always ask why. The answer is usually some version of "Life with a million dollars and no love would still feel empty. But life with great love and only the money I currently have would be very fulfilling!" or "I can always make more money, but I may never find a love like that again."

Now stop and think about how much time you spend in your life every day, week, month and year, to earn money. Think about how much effort you expend and how much stress you are willing to experience in the pursuit of that money. And you do all of this for a dollar amount that is most likely less than a million dollars.

If you picked the relationship option, then you should be willing to put at least as much effort into your love life as your work. When you think about it this way, is the amount of effort you are now putting into your love life versus your work being divvied out appropriately? Is it an equitable balance? Does the amount of time and effort you are currently expending on your respective goals represent your true priorities?

Task Master

Most people go through their entire lives just completing the next task and then the next and so on. Have you really sat down and asked yourself what is most important to you? Have you thought about what will provide you with the most meaning and happiness in your life?

Based on the answer to the love-or-money question, is the amount of effort you are going to have to put into getting dates, interviewing PIPs, and making a relationship work, worth it for you? Does the amount of effort you have been putting into your love life now make sense to you? It is so important that you prioritize and actually make a decision as to how much effort you will put into your love life.

In romance, like everything else in life, you get out what you put in. Having a great love life will require work for the rest of our lives. The work is different when you are in a relationship, but it is still work.

Working on your love life (or relationship) doesn't have to be a horrible thing. Romance just isn't an automatic-pilot thing. Many relationships crash and burn because one or both people involved go on auto-pilot. Next thing you know the whole relationship takes a nosedive.

Once you find that person you *could be* happy with forever, you will still have to expend effort to keep the relationship healthy and strong. Always remember, it's "could be" happy forever, not "will be." We will always need to keep working on ourselves. There is always more to learn and areas in which we can improve ourselves.

The Mechanics of It

Having a marriage or relationship run smoothly through the years is a lot like keeping a car alive. Both require a commitment to regular maintenance, upkeep and repairs. If you neglect or don't maintain your car (relationship) it will not stay in good condition for long. The warranty (or honeymoon stage) only lasts so long.

All cars (relationships) have breakdowns and problems. We then have to make a decision to either fix the one we've got or trade it in for a new one. If the problem is not huge, it makes more sense to work on the car (relationship) we've got. Sometimes we can fix it ourselves. We can use manuals and tools like self-help books, seminars and tapes. Other times we might need the help of a professional.

When making the decision to fix or trade in, we must realize that no matter what model we get if we trade, it will still take work. It will still need maintenance and occasionally break down. Of course, if you find you've got yourself a "lemon," get rid of it!

The best way to avoid getting a lemon is to exercise "due diligence" in terms of researching your options before making a commitment. There are so many makes and models out there, and within each of those, many options to choose from.

Sometimes you may have to give up some of the options that you want in order to get others that are more important to you. For example, power door locks usually mean power windows. If you want leather seats, you might have to spend the extra money for the other luxury amenities that go in the leather seats package. Many strong men who are good at keeping their promises and commitments also tend to be stubborn and willful. Men who are wonderfully free spirited and spontaneous may also tend towards flakiness.

Features that are mutually exclusive with one maker may not be with another. Or you may find that the model that has all of the options you've been looking for doesn't have the horsepower you desire. Bottom line, in order to avoid buyer's remorse, do your shopping and research before you make your final decision and commitment.

Never underestimate the importance of a nice long test drive. A particular car (man) may have all the qualities that are on the list of what you want. However, if it's not fun to drive, you still may choose against it. Likewise, you may test-drive a car (man) that, according to your list, is not what you want, but really makes you happy. So keep your mind open and enjoy shopping.

Try me, Good Lookin'!
Hey Baby, I'm the flavor of the day!
Wooowie!!
Hello!
ACFernandez

Chapter 12
There Is No Such Thing as a Bad Date!

Many people are so frightened of having a bad date or a relationship that does not work out that they stop themselves from going out with anyone who could be flawed in any way. In my philosophy (that being single is one big research project), every situation we get into is a learning experience.

Ice Cream, You Scream

Think of it this way: What if someone introduced you to ice cream for the first time. The flavor, vanilla. MMMM! It's so tasty, you think, "Nothing could taste as good!" Then your friend says, "Now you really must try Chocolate Chip Cookie Dough ice cream!" So you do, and lo and behold, it's even better!

Are you now upset that you wasted your taste buds trying the vanilla? Just because it did not turn out to be the flavor of ice cream you would choose to eat every day for the rest of your life? No, it was still worth tasting.

The more flavors you taste, the more you will learn about what you want and don't want in an ice cream/man. Soon you will start to be able to almost know, just by looking at the package closely (and reading the ingredients), whether or not you are interested in a particular flavor. NO NUTS PLEASE!! I recommend that you not make a final decision without trying at least 31 flavors, just to be sure.

This One's Just Right

Dating is your opportunity to check out all of the available flavors—not just of men, but of relationships. Let me explain. When you have a rotten date or a relationship that ends badly, this is not a bad thing. It is really an opportunity to find out more about how to quickly spot what you want and don't want in a partner.

Working relationships happen when the combination is right. It's not just a question of "is he the right guy," in terms of a laundry list of attributes—it's also about what the dynamic is like between the two of you. I have gone out with one guy who brought out my most stubborn ornery side, while at the same time I was dating another who brought out my sweetest most cooperative side.

Side Note

I am frequently asked if I think there is anything wrong with dating more than one guy at a time. It is only wrong if you are not truthful with everyone involved. Some women say that it does not work for them emotionally. In that case, I say "don't do it." As a rule of thumb, I like to bring up and discuss whether or not we are dating other people very early, so that nobody assumes anything. This is the best way to avoid anyone getting hurt.

Gone Fishin'

Dating is often compared to fishing—you know, "there are more fish in the sea . . ." Here is my Zen fishing/dating philosophy. Many people go fishing with the specific goal of catching fish. If they don't happen to catch any fish that day, they will consider it a bad day. I say they have wasted an incredible opportunity to deeply relax and experience nature.

When I go fishing my goal is to relax and experience nature, and catching fish is a possible bonus. My way, fish or no fish, I had a great day. One of the wisest persons I know, my cousin Elayne, says, "It is best to be in the rainbow for the colors. If there really does turn out to be a pot of gold at the end, that's nice too." (And given the way the price of gold fluctuates, I think she's right.)

When I date, I make it my goal to learn about myself and men—not to fall in love with "The One" and live happily ever after. Therefore every date is a good date. If you do have a date that you feel went "badly," just remember that even if you learned what you don't want, you still learned something. This makes the date worth your time and trouble. There is huge value in knowing and understanding exactly what you are unwilling to accept.

AHernandez

Chapter 13
Two-Headed Beasts

It is incredibly important that we as women study and understand the differences between ourselves and the male of our species. Their minds and anatomy are created and wired together differently than our own. We must understand these differences well and communicate with men accordingly. One of the biggest differences between men and women is that men have two heads!

The Nature of the Beast

We must always be aware that men are only capable of thinking with one head at a time. That is the nature of the beast! If your presentation looks very sexy, you will be talking to the one in their pants. You must understand that men are usually incapable of transferring to the head on top of their shoulders if you began your communications with that lower head. However, if you start with the upper head, you will not have a problem communicating with the lower one when you want its "ATTEN-TION!"

Target Your Market

Your attire should (as they say in the advertising biz) target your market! For those of you who have not heard that phrase before, it means that you design your presentation to interest the specific people you hope to entice. It's like when you go fishing, you find out the favorite food of the particular fish you hope to catch, and use that for bait.

In other words, try to draw attention to the aspect of yourself that you want to be wanted for. As a make-up artist I advise people to use the boldest colors around their best features. That will attract attention to that area—the same way you would highlight in yellow marker the most important part of a written communication to make that part the most noticeable.

Know what is most beautiful about you and then dress to highlight that. For instance, you could highlight your sense of humor, earthy nature, creativity, tenderness, even your femininity. If you are dressed overly sexy, you are highlighting your sexuality. You will then attract men who are looking specifically for sex. Men want super-sexy women for sex; they want a real person for a relationship.

I'm Too Sexy

I wish I had a dime for every scantily clad woman who has complained to me about how men only want "one thing." These frustrated women will say, "He seemed to be such a great guy! I even started to think he was relationship material. But he turned out to be like all the rest, all hands and 'appendages,' and no heart. Men don't want to get to know who a woman really is. They just push and push for sex, and then they never call."

When I hear this, my heart breaks and my mind boggles, because I know why this is happening to them and how to stop it, but it's hard to convince them. The media has incorrectly programmed us that dressing sexy is the way to get a man interested in you. In the movies, the handsome prince falls in love with the maiden with the most cleavage showing.

I used to have the same problem as the women above. Men used to only be able to see my most "obvious" attributes. Now men look at me as a whole person. They see me as someone they want to partner with in every sense of the word, not just the physical. This is because I now understand that men are different than me—so I target my market with my presentation accordingly.

Good Tips

In order to make my point, let me tell you a little story about this horrible waitress who I had the misfortune of being served by (though you could hardly call it service). I overheard her speaking to another waitress when I came out of the restroom. She was complaining that "The big tippers always sit in your section and the lousy tippers always end up in mine!"

It is obvious to the rest of us that this waitress's attitude was creating the lousy tippers. This is because we can all personally relate to getting bad service from a rude waitress and therefore leaving a lousy tip.

But it is not as obvious to us that when we dress overly sexy, we are creating men who only want us for sex. That is because we cannot relate to what happens inside a man's body and mind when he looks at a very sexily dressed woman.

Can You Relate?

Since the first time I realized that I was experiencing PMS (as opposed to being possessed), I have wished that someone would invent a pill that could induce the feelings of PMS. I would slip this pill to men in a drink. (I'd also slip just one to every woman who says, "PMS is nonsense. I never have any problems!") Then they would know what it is really like. If they made a pill that would simulate the way a man's body interferes with his ability to think straight when sexually enticed, I would advise all women take one of those too.

We must understand that when men are aroused, they experience a sexual override that is just as real and uncontrollable as PMS. Please don't misunderstand what I am saying. I am not excusing ANY behavior on men's part. I am saying that they cannot help but feel as they do. It's just like, though we may feel like "going postal" once every 28 days, we are still responsible for not actually going out and killing a couple dozen people with an AK-47.

Men are capable of, and responsible for, controlling their actions. They are not, however, capable of controlling the overwhelming feeling of wanting sex when they see a woman whose apparel advertises it. When that happens, they may not be able to think of anything else.

Man Logic

Generally speaking, when a woman sees a man and thinks OOO-LA-LA, she'll fantasize about him holding her or kissing her or something along those lines. When a man sees a woman that gives him the OOO-LA-LA feeling, his mind goes directly to "plugging her socket!" I mean he literally goes there.

When a man sees a woman dressed super-sexy, he believes she has dressed this way because she is looking to find a man to have sex with her. Often he will turn to his friend and say, "She wants it, *bad!*" The thought of a relationship with this girl never enters his mind. And, according to him, "a relationship is not what she's looking for either."

It took me quite some time to figure men out because my female mind does not work at all this way. I assure you that I have asked many men if I am "getting" how it is for them, and they usually say something like, "Yes. *Duh!*" They usually don't believe me when I say that we women don't all already know this. They consider this to be a totally obvious FACT: "If a woman is dressed sexy and talks sexy, that means she is looking for sex, and only sex." They think that we are dressing sexy as a way to let them know that sex is what we are looking for. They look at it as an unspoken agreement. They think WE are ALL in agreement.

So when a man lays his eyeballs on a woman who "wants it," all power automatically transfers to his lower head. Nature wired men that way. Mama Nature was probably just trying to ensure the continuance of the species. She was aware of how focused man can become on other important things (like football, for instance), so she put in this automatic sexual override.

Dog Meat

If you advertise your sexuality as your best or most obvious feature, don't be surprised if that is all a guy is capable of seeing in you. Likewise, in conversation and flirting, it is a good idea to steer away from sexual innuendo. That is, unless of course a purely sexual interaction is all that you're looking for.

The responsibility of determining the direction of the relationship, unfortunately and unfairly (and yet realistically), falls on the woman. We must be the ones to control whether the relationship will become purely sexual, or whether it will be an emotional *and* sexual relationship.

Asking the guy to do that part is like asking a dog to not eat a raw slab of meat sitting right in front of him. Though you may be able to keep him from taking the meat, you can't stop him from drooling. And no matter what, he won't be able to think of anything else until he has devoured the meat. Also note that he will do anything he has to do in order to get what he wants. (We don't blame the dog for any of this; we know it is just the nature of the beast.)

Even the most wonderful man can fall victim to his nature and his hormones. Especially if the way we are dressed is (a-hem) creating a blood loss from his brain—which happens to be located inside the head we are trying to make contact with.

It is so important to understand that the lower head has no emotion. A man cannot truly make LOVE to a woman without the participation of his mind! Check all of this out with your male friends. Please inform all of your female friends of your findings (especially the young girls in your life). I have avoided so much heartbreak since I figured this stuff out.

Someone Pays the Price

I have come across a few men who are resistant to these notions. They are afraid that if women figure this out, they will stop wearing low-cut shirts and hiked-up skirts. Men enjoy looking at half-dressed women and don't want to be deprived of this free "visual smorgasbord."

These men do not *understand* the price that the women involved are paying. They don't realize that this leads women to emotional pain because men are being so blinded by their "beauty" that they are oblivious to women's souls. When a woman dresses this way, it often leads men to misrepresent how they really feel about her. Men (like doggies) can get into a mode where they will do or say whatever they have to in order to get what they want.

These men may *say* that women dressing sexy is harmless. But on some level they know that what I have said is true. I'll BET ANYTHING that if they have a daughter, they are doing everything within their power to prevent her from dressing sexy!

Too Much Too Soon

If things become too physical too early in a relationship, most men will quickly "turn tail" and run away. This happens even if the man was the one who pushed it to that point. Sex is very intimate for both men and women. Having had it with someone you hardly know or don't have strong feelings for can lead to a feeling similar to embarrassment.

For the man this kind of sex is like a balloon that is filling with helium, taking him higher and higher. When the balloon pops (and the blood starts to flow to his brain again), the light-headed feeling goes away. Now the reality of the inappropriate and intense intimacy starts to set in and he begins to feel uncomfortable.

The most unfair part of this cruel difference is that for most women the act of sex itself usually brings her to the strong feelings that go with the act. The man's balloon is deflating, while the woman's is inflating. The woman's feet leave the ground as the man comes back down to earth.

The Soul-ution

Dress and speak in a way that communicates to his mind and heart only. Resist the temptation to show off your physical attributes to a man in the early stages of a relationship. During this interview stage, show him your heart and mind and allow him to develop his feelings for you based on the strength of those attributes.

Proceed to the other important parts of the anatomy only when you are sure that the relationship is ready. You know that it's probably all right to move forward when you are clear that you and he have had a meeting of the minds and hearts—and that this meeting has gone the way you wanted it to. This means NO "couch wrestling" (until you get to know him better).

Help him to keep his concentration on your *inner* features by not flaunting the ones that "stand out." I'm not in any way suggesting that you try to look unappealing. Be your most beautiful romantic self. Accentuate your *femininity* full-out, but keep your sexuality subtle in the beginning.

Try to target your market. Take me, for example. I want to be loved and appreciated for my uniqueness, my sense of humor and my romantic nature. I want to create a loving partnership with a man. Therefore when I go out I dress accordingly. I will wear something unique (something most people aren't wearing). I will also wear something a little fun or silly (cute earrings or a funny T-shirt). I wear my hair down (long and shiny), very romantic. I do try to look pretty, but not sexy. I look like a real person, a woman a man could picture as his partner. See how I am specifically targeting my market?

The Inside Scoop

How do you know if you are making contact with the head of choice? I put this question to my "inside source" and here is what he said. "When a man is really falling for a woman, initially he almost can't even bear to look at her as a sexual object. Doing so would somehow feel disrespectful. On the other hand, if his intentions are purely sexual, he thinks, 'Come on, what are we waiting for? Let's get down to business!' The test to see if a man is becoming emotionally involved is that, if he is, he will proceed with caution when it comes to sex."

I have interviewed several men on the subject to see if my source and his friends were the norm. Most of them were shocked that I did not already know this stuff. One said, "If a man is falling in love, there is no way he will push the sex thing." They were sure that women knew this and asked me what rock I'd been living under.

Feeling a bit lame, I ran this by some of my smartest female friends. Most of them were as enlightened by this new information as I was. Though when we thought about it, it really did fit. This information explained a lot about each of our past experiences.

Based on these findings, I am now aware of why my own love life has become so much more fulfilling—now that I no longer show off my physical wares until I am sure we already have a relationship.

Men are now seeing me (and liking me) as a whole person. I wonder if that is where the word "wholesome" comes from. Believe me, men are attracted to wholesome women, and they want them for a relationship, not *just* for sex!

You never lose out by showing the "human being" that you are first. Then if all goes well show them the "sexual being" that you are later—again not just with your actions but with your attire, presentation and overall attitude.

SUPERPRUDE!

Able to fend off superficial men
with a single word,
"No!"

Chapter 14
SEX

For the record, I am not at all "easy." In fact I am quite difficult! I am an outright prude, and I advise prudence to all women. I have nothing against sex; in fact, I love it. I don't believe sex between consenting adults (who are not otherwise committed) is ever morally or ethically wrong. I simply believe that having sex too soon is not good for a budding relationship. And I know it is emotionally painful and unfulfilling for me.

Deeply Touched

My theory is that as women, our soul is located in our reproductive center and that during sex, it is touched by the man. When someone I do not know or care deeply about touches my soul, I am depleted. When my soul is touched by someone who I do know and care deeply for, I feel as though my soul has been added to. So I choose only the latter.

For me, the emotional feelings must come first, and be reciprocated. Then comes the wonderful passionate expression of those feelings. I don't have a strong sense of where a man's soul is physically located. I don't think that a man's soul is always touched during sex, which could explain why sex without strong feelings is not necessarily emotionally painful for men. I am glad I am a woman!

Many women who I've expressed these thoughts to have thanked me for putting their feelings into words. A few have said that casual sex is not at all emotionally painful for them and they enjoy it. However, most have also said they can see that by moving too quickly they have "nipped" many potentially good relationships "in the bud."

So many women in both categories have expressed such confusion about how to deal with the issue, that I decided to include it in this book.

Here's How I Deal with It

On the first date, at the first mention of anything even slightly sexual, I say straight out, "By the way, you should know right off—I'm prude." This usually catches a guy off guard, so he will ask me what I mean. I tell him, "I am very slow about getting physical or sexual. I like to take my time and really get to know you before we start getting real passionate, and I want you to know what to expect." I explain that for me being physical is an expression of my feelings for him, and I have to get to know him for a while in order to develop those feelings.

I have had many reactions to this from the men I have gone out with. Interestingly, I have found it to be a good way to see just what kind of man I'm dealing with. If a guy in any way invalidates or belittles my feelings, or the way I expressed them, he clearly does not respect me. There have been a few men who have responded negatively to my statement. The ones I have continued to date have shown me that this is not the only situation where they are going to disrespect my feelings.

Most men, however, are actually impressed with my candor and pleased with my stance. I would say it makes them think more seriously about me. It usually ends up making them like me more, though it is in no way a manipulation. That is one of the best things about expressing yourself honestly. If the guy accepts it, he accepts YOU.

Best of all, if things do progress to a sexual relationship, the man knows that he is really special to me. We have already established that sex means something and that taking this step moves the relationship to a new level. This takes away that post-coital confusion, angst and fear, and leaves room for basking in the afterglow.

Don't get me wrong, I'm all for talking about it later if there is any question that we are still "on the same page." Things can get really iffy after that big step. Which is another reason why I like to wait. It takes time to establish good enough communication in order to deal with any shock waves that having sex for the first time may cause.

Regrets Suck

I do know of relationships that worked out even though the couple slept together early on. Most of these couples will say it like that—"even though," meaning that "we worked out despite the fact that we had sex very early." They will say, "We got past it."

Please understand that I am not making a judgment here. Always do what ever works for you!! Just be clear that if a man cares for you, your decision to wait, if that *is* what works for you, WILL NOT TURN HIM OFF!! More likely, it will turn him on.

You rarely hear people in relationships say, "I just wish we had slept together sooner." Even men will say, "I'm glad we waited." So it makes sense to err on the side of waiting. If he cares for you, the sex will still be there tomorrow. Having sex too soon does not make a man have stronger feelings for a woman, EVER.

Do You Remember the First Time?

I also want to give you the advice I give to the young women in my life: You only get to do anything for the first time once. The first kiss is always the most special and exciting. The same goes for all of the other bases.

If you have already made it all the way to "home base" in your life, then you will not get the opportunity to experience more of those incredibly magical "first times" again. But, you do have the opportunity to experience that magical first-time feeling again (to some extent) with any new man in your life.

I say, savor each new "first time" one at a time. Why rush? If you do it all in one night, or even one week, then it's all done. Think of how special each of those moves will be if this man does end up being "The One." You will want to remember each one of them for the rest of your life.

Also keep in mind that if you get your wish, and this man and you do end up living happily ever after together, you will never again get the opportunity to experience any of those magical "firsts." That is, of course, a fair trade-off.

Nonetheless, every "first" is something special to be slowly savored, thoroughly experienced, and clearly remembered. This is hard to do if you are nervous or rushing through all of them in one night, so slow down and enjoy!

My Bottom-Line Advice

Only do what you feel great about doing! Gently, clearly and honestly tell the guy exactly what to expect, even if it feels uncomfortable in the moment. TAKE HIS REACTION AS INFORMATION ABOUT HIM, NOT YOU!

Chapter 15
Soul Searching

I'd be one rich chicky if I had a dollar for every woman who has complained to me that "Men are always unfairly discriminating against dating women based on their looks!" Women say that men only want gorgeous, perfect-bodied, young, Barbie Doll, *Baywatch*-looking women. They tell me that men do not look at what is really important in a woman, what's on the inside. Many of these women cite this as the biggest obstacle standing between them and the love life they desire.

Whether you personally have this complaint or not, you can see that if this is true of men, it is unfair of them. We can all agree that men should look at what a wonderful soul we have. They should value us based on how supportive, loving, kind, sensitive, smart, honest and fun we are, and so forth.

Now, if I had another dollar for every woman who has voiced the above complaint and has also told me about some wonderful man who she won't date because she "just isn't attracted to him," I would be almost twice as rich! *Seriously!*

Is That Fair?

When I hit these women with this injustice, they will often say, "Men are not going to stop unfairly discriminating based on looks, so why should we?" My answer: When men discriminate in this way they are not just hurting women, they are hurting themselves. They are bypassing wonderful women every day that could be making them blissfully happy. And all because the outer shell is not decorated the way they want. Do *we* want to make this same foolish mistake, just because men may not stop making it?

Here is a choice for you. You can either have the most attractive man you can imagine—we are talking Mel Gibson meets Tom Cruise (or who ever gets your motor running). This man, however, is not supportive, kind, honest, or accepting of you. Your other choice is a mediocre-looking to "UG-O" man who loves you dearly for who you really are. He is kind, gentle, supportive, and strong, with a high level of integrity. He is all that is most important to you, but he does not "float your boat" in the looks department. Which would you choose?

Shell-Shocked

If you won't even date a guy unless his shell meets your criteria, you are being unfair to yourself and to him. You are also being closed-minded, superficial, and possibly a hypocrite. I am sorry to beat you so profusely on this one, but I can't stand to see women keeping themselves from something they so desire for such an unfair and illogical reason.

Many of the women who are so determined to date only "Hot Toddies" are themselves not "Perfect 10s." So if men won't bend and women won't bend...they are both making an unconscious decision to remain alone, rather than look inside the shell, to the soul of a person. The result is a lot of unnecessarily lonely hearts.

Think about the people that you love most in the world, your favorite friends and family. Wouldn't you love them even if they were "butt-ugly"? Wouldn't you still see their inner beauty?

Happily Ever After

Let's say you meet and fall in love with a handsome man. He is your soul mate. You get married and have kids and are happily-ever-aftering. Then one day he becomes disfigured in some terrible accident. Is it over now that his shell has become unappealing to you?

I ask that question to any woman who fights me on this whole "looks" thing. Almost every single one says, "Well, of course if we were married I would stick by him. In that circumstance it wouldn't change my feelings towards him." Yes, this is totally logical. However, don't you see that you may be passing up your soul mate because he wasn't *born* in the package you expected?

You wouldn't give up your soul mate if his package changed, but if it starts out that way he's disqualified. You must realize what you are saying. You are willing to give up your soul mate and a potentially incredible relationship, based on your standard of beauty.

Do you want a man to judge you based on your outside appearance? Good or bad, don't you want him to look past the shell to the inside? Don't you feel like the modern vision of "beautiful" is way too narrow and unfair to the average woman? Don't you think that unattractive people deserve love too? What if YOU were born ugly? Wouldn't you still be the wonderful, unique and deserving person that you are?

No Fairy Tale

Here is my personal story of how I came to a place where I stopped discriminating against men based on looks. Growing up, I had what you might call a long awkward stage. It started when I was about seven and lasted until about 17. Finally the ugly duckling turned into a kind of attractive ducky. I know you were hoping for a swan—so was I, at the time.

Needless to say, my self-esteem had to catch up to my appearance. As soon as I got a little confidence, I learned how to play the "Aloof/Hard-to-Get Game" incredibly well.

The aloof game is most effective on men who want what they can't have. Usually these are really good-looking men who can get any woman they want. These men become bored of women always throwing themselves at them. They begin to look for more of a challenge. Soon I was dating the "cream of the crop," the best-looking, most sought-after men.

Given that in the past I was unable to get any dates at all, this was quite satisfying. At least at first it was. As time went on, it became heartbreaking. You see, if you make the mistake of falling in love with the kind of man who only wants what he can't have, he will quickly fall out of love with you. Because he now "has you" and you are no longer hard to get, the challenge and the magic disappears for him. POOF! *Ouch, that hurts!*

"Well," I thought, "I know how to solve that problem." So I got really good at NOT falling in love with them. Even though my strategy worked and I was now able to keep these highly sought-after men wanting me, this was even less fulfilling. Finally, I began to question why their looks were so important to me.

Leggo' My Ego!

I realized that it was all about my ego. My ego had deduced, "If these men who could have any woman they wanted, chose me, then I must be something special." Then suddenly I had the horrible realization that the reason they wanted me wasn't really about me anyway. It was just that I was better at playing this awful game than the other women they had come across. *YUCK!*

I then became very interested in what a real relationship would be like. You know, one where the guy loved me for my true self, as opposed to my ability to resist going goo-goo over him. A relationship where I loved the man for who he is and not because he made me appear more special.

I made a decision right then and there that I would never again disqualify a man based on his looks. That decision has served me well. Now thinking any other way seems totally illogical to me.

Don't Just Take My Word for It

Many friends and clients have said things like this to me: "If I don't feel an attraction or chemistry for a man, there is no way I can have a relationship with him." Personally I have found that as I get to know someone, if I like him I become attracted to him and the chemistry begins to build.

Many friends and clients, now in happy, loving and fulfilling relationships, have found that when they gave it a chance the same has happened for them. Here is the story of one woman who represents many women I personally know. We will call her Katie.

I always ask my hair clients, "How's your love life?" Katie had come in for her haircut with the same story four times in a row. She said she was lonely and tired of it. She had a few false starts with men she was extremely attracted to, but they proved to be unhealthy choices for her.

Katie kept talking about this one guy who was very nice and very interested in her. But, she said that he just didn't "do it for her." She just was not attracted to him.

Every time she came in, I would relay stories to her of other women who overcame their "looks discrimination" thing, and were now living happily ever after. I described how I myself have developed strong attractions for men who at first glance were outright unappealing to me.

I have to give Katie a lot of credit. She was so resistant to the concept of going out with someone she was not attracted to, in order to see if an attraction would build. It was particularly difficult for her to buy into what I was saying. She, being a very beautiful woman, had never been on the receiving end of looks discrimination. She could not relate to the pain that is involved.

Every month she would try so hard to open herself to this sweet man's affection. I was elated when she came in one time and told me she had started seeing him. Since then, every time I've seen her she's been more and more in love with this wonderful man.

Katie will now tell you that she is more attracted to this man than any other before him. She explains how amazing it was, once she gave in. The more she got to know him, the more she started to notice how handsome he is. She also claims that this is the healthiest, most romantic relationship she's ever been in.

Just Add Water

I have found that the "instant chemistry" usually results in more pain than pleasure for me. I think it's because what I am actually attracted to is some sort of negative excitement. This is probably based on some unhealthy baggage from my childhood (mine is monogrammed). Or it could be my own dangerous kind of "wanting-what-I-can't-have" thought process.

Even though I am not exactly sure what that "instant" attraction *is* based on, I definitely know it's *not* based on who the man really is. There is no way I could possibly know who he is, yet. I can only learn that in time.

I do believe that love at first sight is possible. You could look at someone and see directly into their soul, and fall forever in love. I also think we can have a similar feeling when it is really this negative attraction. The best way to find out which one it is, is to take your time and find out. If it is true love, you will have all the time you need.

Women often ask me, "So, how do you recommend I decide who to date and who not to date?" The answer is simple: Allow the man to disqualify himself. Sometimes the relationship will disqualify itself. Decide what is most important to you, and what is unacceptable to you, and then qualify men accordingly.

For instance, if a guy shows himself to be rude, mean, dishonest, or if he does not accept and support me, he disqualifies himself for me. The relationship disqualifies itself if we are incompatible, or if mutual love or mutual respect does not develop.

I Double-Dog Dare Ya

I challenge you to take on the following: For the next six months, you only disqualify a man for things he is capable of controlling. (Control does not include being surgically altered.)

Hairlines and waistlines are in different departments. He *can* control his waistline. If he has bad breath, that's a fair reason to say,

"Sorry, Charlie." If he has an ugly face, you still give him a go. If his personal hygiene leaves something to be desired, it's fair to leave him behind. If he has no behind (believe me, that is not within his control), he still gets a chance.

If he is rude to a waitress, does not open your door, or when the bill arrives hands it to you (assuming you don't approve of this), you can dump him. In other words, you will only disqualify a man based on what is really important to you, other than his outward appearance or shell.

Kissing Frogs

See how you feel after six months. Of course, you may be madly in love with an incredible human being by then. You may have found your soul mate. You could be well on your way to living happily ever after with a prince that at first glance appeared to be a frog.

The funny thing is, all of your single friends will say, "You're so lucky to have found Prince Froggy! You have no idea how hard it is to be out there picking from all of these egocentric, narcissistic men!"

It is true, by the way, that once a couple is happily in love, nobody cares about their looks anymore anyway. When people hear that someone is married, you rarely hear them ask, "How good-looking is her husband?" We usually ask, "What is her husband like? Is she happy, does he treat her well?" Why is this? Because that is what is really important, and we all know it.

Just recently I was people watching when I noticed this couple who were obviously deeply, madly and passionately in love. The woman was beautiful. The man was not at all "friendly on the sockets" (eyeballs). It is a rare thing for me to feel the strong envy I felt toward these incredibly happy love birds looking deeply into each others eyes. I also felt like going and giving the woman a high five.

Do You Eat Sushi?

We are often the same way with food as we are with men. If the food doesn't look attractive, we don't want to taste it. I say, "Try it, you might like it!" If you don't like it, you can always spit it out and never eat it again.

If you are closing yourself off to something without ever having tried it, you are not being fair to yourself. I was shocked to find out I love spinach soufflé, and it took me till age 30 to try sushi! I really hope that you will open your mouth, and your mind.

The Nose Knows

One final tidbit I want you to consider: Many men who are extremely attractive often have developed little else to offer a woman in a relationship. They can sometimes be superficial and fickle. Of course unattractive men can also be this way, so how do we avoid these men?

I have a big nose. I used to hate it, but now it's my best friend. It acts as a filter to keep totally superficial men from wanting me. Whatever flaw you have, can work for you in the same way. My nose is just bad enough to keep away the men who are *only* looking for "arm candy" (something to decorate their arm). I want a man who likes the way I look, but not as the "meat" of his feelings for me—my looks should be the dessert!

Section IV
Obstacle Course In-Sight

Chapter 16
Self-Fulfilling Prophecies

This is one of the most important chapters in this book, and not just for improving your love life. You can use the technology I am about to describe in every aspect of your life! I believe that self-fulfilling prophecies not only are real, but can actually be used as a tool. Whether you know it or not, you are probably already using this tool in your daily life.

Unfortunately, most of the time when this tool is used unknowingly, it is used in a destructive way—often demolishing one's love life like a sledgehammer. Many women who have taken my seminars have told me that this segment was the single most powerful piece of information they received.

Not everyone believes that self-fulfilling prophecies have power. Some people may say, "There is probably something to it, but I don't really think it's a big deal." No matter what you think of self-fulfilling prophecies, I have a request. For the sake of this discussion I ask that you suspend any skepticism you may feel on the subject, just long enough for me to make my point.

No Sale Is Ever Final

If, when I am finished, you believe that what I am saying is at all possible, then I also ask that you try using this technology for one month. If it works for you, stay with it. Please keep in mind that this technology only works if you truly believe that it will. Therefore, in order to try it out, you will have to psych yourself into really believing it for that time period.

People are often confused by my use of the word "technology" in this instance. The definition of technology is "applied science." The word "apply" means to use practically or specifically, as when we apply knowledge to a problem. And "science" refers to a branch of knowledge concerned with establishing and systematizing principles and methods by experiments and hypothesis. I say that when we turn self-fulfilling prophecies into a tool, we are "applying" a "science" (systematized principles) to our lives.

"Technology" is the perfect word for the concept I am about to unfold and dissect.

What Is a Self-Fulfilling Prophecy?

Self-fulfilling prophecies can be difficult to describe. You may already know or have a sense of what they are. Still, I want to try to explain exactly what I mean, to be sure we are "on the same page."

A self-fulfilling prophecy occurs when a person has a belief that things will go a certain way, and then they do. I'm not talking about a belief like "I believe the sun will come up tomorrow." I am taking about beliefs like "Everyone seems to be in a bad mood this week!" or "You only find a man when you don't want one!" or "Corporations never promote from within!" These expectations then become a reality in the life of the person who believes them. Meanwhile, the person who believes that the opposite is true has a completely different experience.

We can all see that if people had the above beliefs, and if self-fulfilling prophecies do have power, those people would be setting up a negative reality for themselves. They would be creating fates that they would probably prefer not to create. Obviously, these people do not think they have any control over these things. I believe they are wrong.

If self-fulfilling prophecies do have power, then how or why do they work? Here are three possible explanations for this phenomenon. I am sure there are more, but these are the three that I have come up with so far.

The Filter

The first reason why self-fulfilling prophecies work is what I call the "filter." This is how the filter works.

> *We see and hear through the filter of our beliefs and expectations, and look and listen for what we already "know" (think) will happen.*

We therefore notice what we expected to notice. The more we see what we expected to see, the deeper the belief becomes—which only makes us more convinced that we were right, and a vicious cycle is born.

This would explain an experience that many people can relate to. Have you ever heard a word and noticed that you had never heard it before? Then all of a sudden you start to hear that word all the time. You know that people did not just start using this word because you found out about it. You ask your friends if they have ever heard that word and they are all familiar with it. So what's the deal?

Another example of this filter concept happens to a lot of us when we begin shopping for a car. We may become aware of a particular model that we never really noticed before. Now all of a sudden we begin to see this car everywhere, all the time. Maybe we never "saw" it before because we were not *expecting* to see it.

The "Right" Reason

The second possible reason why self-fulfilling prophecies work is that we are committed to being right. We human beings are an egotistical bunch—not some of us, all of us. This is not necessarily a bad thing, but it can have its downside. (Our commitment to "being right" is usually not a conscious choice.)

> *Because of our ego's commitment to "being right" we will choose the people, situations and circumstances that will comply with our belief.*

This aspect of human nature works in our favor in many ways. A commitment to being right will have us move forward and succeed in our lives. When I was 20 years old and decided I could start my own business, everyone said that I couldn't do it. Because I was committed to being right, I did whatever I had to do to make my business fly. If I didn't mind being wrong, I would have quit any number of times when it seemed impossible to succeed.

Our commitment to "being right" works against us when we are being right about things that aren't good for us. For instance, "I never meet quality men," or "I am no good at flirting." We then do what we need to do to feed our ego, we will choose the people and circumstances that will prove us right. Our ego is more committed to having us "be right" than to having us get what we want in life. Notice, however, that this mechanism is the same exact one that drives us to succeed. For instance, it is what gives us the strength to pull an all-nighter to complete an important project. WE want to sleep, our EGO wants to "be right" (about us succeeding).

I have a highly intelligent cousin that I was explaining this to and she said, "Felicia, what you're saying is not true for me because what ever I say is going to happen specifically does not happen. I think when you say what you want to have happen out loud you jinx it. At least that is how it *always* works for me." I tried to convince her that she was committed to "being right" about the "jinx" part and the "always" part. Her response was something on the order of, "It's not that, this is just the way it IS for me." We agreed to disagree.

Far-Out

The third possibility for why self-fulfilling prophecies work might seem a little far-out to those of you who only believe what you can see and touch. If you think this way, then hopefully the first two reasons worked well for you. But please, try to open your mind and accept the following.

> *The universe actually responds to our expectations. Our fate and our circumstances will actually change to comply with our beliefs and expectations.*

If that seems totally weird to you, that's okay. You don't have to believe that this is how self-fulfilling prophecies work. In order to try this technology, you only have to believe that self-fulfilling prophecies do have power. Being open to the possibility that the universe responds to our expectations can't hurt, though. So come on, give it a chance.

You can't see or touch air and yet you thoroughly believe that it exists. There was a time when everybody thought the world was flat, and Chris Columbus was a nutcase with a death wish. More and more people started to get it that the world was spherical, and now those who think we live on a big pancake are the wacky ones. More and more people are starting to believe that the universe responds to our expectations.

If you have religious convictions that this concept conflicts with, I want you to know that I do not wish to invalidate or disrespect any of your beliefs. On the contrary, I deeply respect them. What I have said here is just what works for me. In my mind this concept and God are not mutually exclusive—one does not negate the other. If this concept does not work for you for any reason, please just ignore it. That goes for any of my opinions or ideas in this book or otherwise.

D. All of the Above

Personally, I think self-fulfilling prophecies work for all of the three above reasons. I think that when we believe something is true, we filter everything we experience through our beliefs and look for what we expect. I also think we are committed to "being right" about what we believe and therefore drive those beliefs into reality. And I think the universe responds to our beliefs and creates what we expected. It is a huge, overwhelming force that none of us can resist.

If this is true, then how do we overcome it? We don't! We work with it. We use self-fulfilling prophecies like a tool by choosing only beliefs that will work in our favor. Many people firmly believe that you can not control your thoughts, others say you absolutely can. Here is how I see it:

You cannot *not* think what you think. You cannot stop thinking what you are thinking. I'll prove it to you. Don't think of pickles...didn't that make you think of pickles? Now the harder you try to not think of pickles, the more you will think of them.

The only way that you can now not think of pickles is to think of something else. For instance, if you begin to think of cheesecake, now you can stop thinking of pickles. If you are now thinking of pickles and cheesecake, I apologize. That was not a nice thing for me to do to you.

The point is this: Though you can't make a particular thought go away, you *can choose to add* any thoughts you like. To use self fulfilling prophesies to your advantage, like a "power-tool," you must choose your expectations and beliefs carefully. *Purposely believe and expect the things that you want to have happen.*

The solution will be spelled out in great detail in the next chapter "Power-Tools!" But before can we fix something we must take it apart, dismantle all of the pieces, and understand it's complexities, only then can we put it all together and make it run smoothly.

Let's Take a Closer Look

I will now give you some very clear illustrations of how self-fulfilling prophecies can mess with our life. Let's say someone tells you that people are going to be in a bad mood this week, and you believe them. Maybe they say, "It's because the eighth moon is in the seventh house." If this made sense to you and you took on the same belief, you would then begin to notice all the people you came across who were really moody.

Obviously, at any given time there are some people who are short-tempered and some who are light-hearted. We are hyper-aware of what we expect to happen actually happening. We would notice the people we came across who were in a bad mood and ignore those in a good mood, because that fits with our expectation.

Furthermore, if you think that everyone is in a bad mood, "everyone" includes you. You may bring on a psychosomatic bad mood of your own. Obviously, if you are in a bad mood when you interact with people, they are likely to react by joining you. Can you see how the prophecy that "people will be in a bad mood" fulfills itself?

If we were committed to being right about this, we would pick the people and circumstances that would comply. For instance, if we took that belief to the market, we could subconsciously purposely choose the cashier with a scowl on her face in order to be right. Or we might start to push people's buttons. Then they would get nasty with us and we would again get to be right.

As a side note, I am not saying that I don't believe that the position of the planets can have an effect on our emotions. I always have other people read my horoscope first so that if it is negative, they can tell me not to read it. I always want to know that I did not add to a negative situation by expecting it. I enjoy reading my horoscope the next day. This way, if something did go wrong the previous day I can blame it on the galaxy.

Wronged by Right

This next example gets more specific as to how negative self-fulfilling prophecies can wreak havoc on romance. We will usually go far out of our way to be right. Sometimes we will literally go against our own best interest in order to be right. We may subconsciously choose the people and circumstances that will prove we were right, even when it undermines what we really want.

I will now share with you how my commitment to being right wrecked my love life for years. I once had this belief: "A man would be crazy about a woman until she fell for him, and then he would immediately lose interest in her."

During the time when I had that belief (or should I say, while it had me), it would never fail. I could walk into a room, smoky and dark with hundreds of men in it, and pick out the one guy who would do that to me in a second flat. He would also be the guy that I was most attracted to. I would always "get my man." He would be crazy about me until I fell for him, and then he would lose interest. See, I would be right. What a horrible thing to be right about. Right?

What I want for you to see here is that because I (like all

human beings) was committed to "being right," the same thing kept happening to me. This felt like my belief about men was being proven over and over to be true. Therefore, there was no point in even looking for another possibility for why things kept happening this way. So I kept "being right" and the cycle became more vicious.

Finally I became aware that "WE BELIEVE OUR REALITY INTO EXISTENCE." I began to wonder if this was the case with my "man thing." I opened my mind to the idea that I was not right about all men being this way. I then began to look for other reasons why all the men that I was coming across were that way.

Wrong Doing

One of my favorite quotes is, "Insanity is doing the same thing over and over, and expecting a different result." Here is how I stopped ruining my love life by "being right." First I started to force myself to believe differently. I psyched myself into the belief that some men like women who like them. Then I started choosing men differently. At first I just chose men who I would not have chosen before.

That is when I realized that playing aloof and "hard-to-get" attracted only men who wanted an "aloof" woman. My true nature is not at all aloof. I suddenly saw that what had been happening to this point was this: When I would fall for a guy, then the "real" available and affectionate Felicia would begin to show through. My fake-out "aloof" Felicia had attracted a man who would not like the "real" available and affectionate me.

So, I began to show men that I liked them in the very beginning. This way if a guy was the kind of man that only "wants what he can't have," he would not want me right from the start. I would not fall in love and end up hurt because a relationship would not even get past the first hurdle.

I also realized that because my belief was so strong that "if I fell for a guy, he would lose interest in me," when I would start to fall for a guy, I would also start to panic. It is now so clear to me that this panic would cause me to lose my confidence (what originally attracted him to me). I would also begin to feel anger towards the guy for what "I knew he was about to do." I am now sure that the men involved could feel this anger and were confused by it, and turned off by it.

I figured it all out, shifted accordingly, and lo-and-behold, a different reality came to be. Now the men I go out with like me more for liking them. I had been wrong about men. The funny thing is that even though I was now getting what I wanted, I still really disliked the feeling of having been "wrong." The feeling of "being wrong" almost hurts (our ego gets bruised)—even when it means that we get what we want, we don't like the feeling. That also falls under the heading of "Human Nature."

What Do YOU Know?

People would rather "be right" about what is wrong in their life, than "be wrong" and get what they want. We can usually see this clearly in others when we make a suggestion of how to fix an ongoing problem of theirs. They will say, "You just don't understand how it is."

Most of us think, "I'm not that way!" But watch yourself closely—we are all susceptible to our human nature. Remember that our commitment to being right also often works in our favor. We just need to be aware of when it is not. *Any negative belief that we maintain keeps us stuck!*

So often, I hear women "being right" about things that are contradictory to what they want. Here is a list of some of the most popular negative self-fulfilling prophecies that I hear women say about men and why they can't find love: (Underline any you have ever said).

- Men are animals. (Dogs, pigs, you name it.)
- Men only want beautiful, perfect-bodied, young, Barbie Doll, *Bay Watch* women!
- Men—no matter what they look like—think they can get these women, so they hold out and don't give less-than-perfect-looking woman a chance.
- There are no good men in LA! (Fill in the name of the city where you live.)
- All the good ones are taken! (Married, buried or gay.)
- Men are commitment-phobic.
- Men are self-absorbed and/or narcissistic!
- Men are insensitive creeps!
- The ratio of men to women in my area or age group makes it impossible for me to find love.
- Men don't look at what is really important in a woman, what is on the inside.
- Men are *dirty, rotten, cheating scoundrels*. (Or any mistrust statements.)
- There are no quality men left.
- I meet men, but they don't ask me out.

- I don't have time to date.
- I don't know how to flirt.
- Dating sucks!
- I only attract weirdos, or losers, or jerks, or alcoholics, or geeks! (Or any other negative type that you may say you attract.)
- I don't meet/know any quality men.
- Men are not attracted to me because I'm too...old, young, quiet, loud, poor, rich, powerful, weak, active, couch potato, attractive, unattractive, tall, short, big, small, religious, non-religious, smart, simple, complicated, shy, outgoing, party girl, home-body, want too much or not enough sex. (I could go on and on, but I think you catch my drift.)

Some of these may be extreme versions of a belief you may have. It is a good idea to take a moment and write a list of any of the above that fit for you, and any others of your own that I did not list. Look to see what destructive beliefs you have about yourself or men that you could be filtering through, "being right" about, and "creating into the universe" with your expectations.

Can you see that if you are "being right" about any of these things, then there is no point in even trying to look for another reason why your love life is not going the way you want? There would also be no point in trying anything new or different. If any of the above statements were "true" (or right), then it would be hopeless. Do you see how this stops you?

If it is true that you are committed to being right, then you are actually invested in keeping things as they are. Trust me. Nothing on that list is *really* true. *If you believe that something is TRUE you are solidifying that reality for yourself.*

If you find yourself saying, "But it is true!" then you must realize that these negative self-fulfilling prophecies feed on themselves. It's like arguing about what came first, the chicken or the egg. You cannot know what *will* happen, or what *all* men are like. You can only know what *has* happened with the men you have encountered so far.

For instance, if you say, "I'm in a dating dry spell," although you may have experienced a lapse between dates, the moment you uttered those words you set that reality into motion. Now you are "filtering through," committed to "being right" about, and creating that "dry spell" for yourself.

You have just witnessed the birth of a negative self-fulfilling prophecy. The dry spell then becomes insidious. And every time you say, "I'm in a dry spell," you solidify, prolong and intensify it. I have known women to get stuck in that one for years on end.

Chapter 17
Power-Tools!

As I said in the last chapter, self-fulfilling prophesies can be used as a tool. When they are being used unknowingly they are usually being used like a sledgehammer, demolishing one's love life. In this chapter we will learn how to use them like a power tool, custom building the love life we desire with speed and accuracy!

Thought Control

Here is how we turn negative self fulfilling prophesies around and then make them work in our favor. First you must realize that the way we think is habitual. Our mind likes to take the same route it took before. The trick is to purposely choose a different route. You decide to think a thought that works better for you. Then you consciously think it over and over until this new route becomes the way your mind is used to going.

To create this new good habit you will need some *positive* self-fulfilling prophecies to believe, filter through, "be right" about and create in the universe with your expectations. Here are some that may work for you. Feel free to steal mine and make up some of your own.

- There are plenty of quality men.
- I meet quality men all the time, everywhere!
- Quality men are attracted to me.
- Men see me for all of my incredible beauty, inside and out.
- I am always being asked out by quality men.
- Quality men want to have a relationship with me.
- I am great at flirting.
- I am great at making people feel comfortable around me.
- Quality men love to be around me.
- It's raining quality men.
- So many quality men want me to go out with them that I have to make time for them all.

AND THE "BE ALL, END ALL":

- Quality men go to sleep each night and wake up every morning hoping to meet a woman like ME!

If that last one is not easy for you to wrap your mind around, don't worry. Once you do the exercise found in the chapter "The Lock-Pick Set," you will be clear that *you are* exactly the kind of woman quality men hope for.

These positive self-fulfilling prophecies are also known as "affirmations." You can change any of the words if something else would work better for you. I want to warn you away from negatives, though. For instance, if you say, "Men are not dogs" the subconscious cannot distinguish the negative. It translates that sentence to "men are dogs." Another example, is if you were to say, "I am not weak," that would translate into "I am weak." It would be more effective to say, "I am strong!" You want to keep your affirmations in the positives. There is no telling what a double negative like "I am no longer attracting bad men" translates to. Just say, "I attract all quality men."

Another important point is that you want to be sure to say your affirmations in the present tense. Your subconscious only know that "later" is not "now." It does not know when to start putting a later statement into effect. You can say, "I now meet tons of quality men." Or, "I meet tons of quality men."

One last helpful hint about affirmations: Sometimes when life is going the worst, which is when you need your affirmations the most, that is when they are the hardest to believe. In those times use this affirmation:

"My affirmations work for me whether I believe they will or not!"

Isn't that a great one? I got that out of a workshop led by Chelly Campbell, called "Financial Stress Reduction." I highly recommend her book by the same name. Sometimes I have to say that affirmation in between each one of mine.

Affirmative Action

Affirmations work for the exact same reasons that self-fulfilling prophecies do. We begin to make these new positive beliefs a reality in our life by filtering through them, "being right" about them and by expecting them. In order to make these things come true in your life, say your affirmations daily. Also say them in your car, and as you are falling asleep. Say them out loud and in your mind as often as possible.

Some people find it effective to write them down on a piece of paper and tape it to their mirror. They read them every time they pass them by and when they are getting ready to go out, to work, or

Quality Men are ALWAYS attracted to me.

I am great at making people feel comfortable around me.
AFernandez

to bed. Others will write their affirmations on many pieces of paper and put them all over the place. Do whatever works to keep them in the forefront of your mind.

I have a tendency to read one thing and think another. So I have to write down my affirmations daily, or anytime I catch myself thinking negatively. I never copy from the day before, so I have to generate the positive thoughts newly every time. I have found that my affirmations are more effective if I have to think of them out of my brain, rather than just copy them from another piece of paper.

This is the way that works best for me. I keep my "Affirmations Work!" book next to my bed, and use a new page each night. I affirm that I can and will handle well, whatever I plan to do the next day. I acknowledge myself for all "jobs well done." I tell myself wonderful things about me. I undo any negative thoughts that have come up that day. I also predict that the specific things I am hoping will happen, will.

"Affirmations Work!" Book

I am often asked to describe more specifically the way that I do this. Here is a specific example that will illustrate my method. When I was looking for a publisher for this book (a feat many said was basically impossible for an unpublished writer), I wrote this every night: "The perfect publisher for my book and I will find each other very soon. The universe is now setting up that meeting." I would then describe that publisher in detail. Then I wrote, "I will say the perfect words, to the perfect publisher, so that the publisher will recognize that my book is a wise choice." All of that has already happened.

I also wrote, and still write, "*Master Dating* will be a huge success and make a huge powerful positive difference in the lives of millions!!!" This remains to be seen, though I believe the wheels are already set in motion. Every time I write this, my heart skips a beat. Even good changes are scary. Affirming the changes that you want to take place gives you the opportunity to begin to digest them. This way you can get out of your own way and allow them to happen.

When I am ready to meet the perfect guy for me, and give up being single, I will do similar affirmations about him. I have to be sure that I am ready, because I usually meet a new boyfriend within a week of starting to affirm him. (What you just read is also an affirmation—one that is now easy for me to believe because it has been proven to me in the real world. But I assure you that the affirmation came first.

See how it works?)

One last thing that I want to say about affirming something into your life: When you describe what you want, it is important to be as specific as possible. However, sometimes we do not know exactly what is best for us. For this reason I will always add to the end of my affirmations, "or whatever is perfect for me!" This way the universe will create what is truly best for me, above and beyond what I think is best.

Think About What You Think About

It is important to begin to really notice what you think. Do not try to edit what you THINK; that would be denial. It is a good idea to edit what you SAY. When we say something out loud or write something down, that solidifies it in our mind. This also puts the wheels in motion to fulfill it like a prophecy.

This is what you should do anytime you catch yourself saying a negative statement or having a negative thought: First, acknowledge that what you just said/thought was a negative self-fulfilling prophesy. Next tell yourself, "That the statement/thought is not true." Then undo it with three positives that *specifically* counteract that negative. Do this anytime you have a thought that, if it were true, would not get you what you want in life.

Here is an example of how it works:

Negative: "I just don't seem to meet any quality men."

1. Catch yourself.
2. Acknowledge that this is a negative self-fulfilling prophecy.
3. Tell yourself, "This is not true."
4. Then correct yourself by saying something like, "In the past I did not seem to run into quality men."
5. Next, think of and say three things that specifically counteract the negative. Here are three that would work to counteract this negative:

- "I now meet quality men all the time."
- "Quality men are showing up everywhere I go."
- "Quality men are attracted to me and make themselves known to me regularly."

Try a few of your own so you know you are getting the hang of it. Take as much time as you need. I suggest that you do the entire process on paper just the way I laid it out. If not, at least say the process out loud in order to solidify it. Finding even one positive that

Quality men go to sleep and wake up everyday hoping to meet a woman like me.
ooo

counteracts the negative is usually not easy. If you can only think of one positive, it's okay to say the same one three times. But try to change it around a little bit each time you say it.

Remember that since you have had these negative thoughts for quite some time, they may not be easy habits to break. We must be diligent in noticing negative thoughts when they come up. We must be consistent with our three counteractive thoughts, in order to create the new habit. If you do keep this up, it will not only become easier and easier, it will eventually become automatic more often than not.

Soon you will naturally and habitually think positively most of the time. Then you will start to filter through, "be right" about them, and magically generate these new, purposely self-generated, positive beliefs into your life on a regular basis.

The Luck of the Draw

By the way, luck is also created. It works in the same way as self-fulfilling prophecies. I have always been an incredibly lucky person. I believe it is because I always say, "I am an incredibly lucky person!" (I haven't always known that the reason I was so lucky was because I always say "I'm so lucky.")

Many people I have told this to, have resisted it initially. Then I convince them to give it a try. Those who said they were able to really take on the belief that "they are lucky" said that they began having good luck too.

Talk to Yourself

Use this technology (apply this science) whenever you are getting ready to go on a date, to a party, or anyplace where you think you might meet PIPs. As you are getting dressed and doing your hair and make-up, start to affirm that there will be quality men where you are going. Tell yourself that you will meet those quality men and be attracted to them. Assure yourself that any quality man that sees you will immediately recognize you as a quality woman and will also be attracted to you.

On the ride to your destination, go over these thoughts and any other positive thoughts you can add to these. Mentally keep it up once you have arrived. As this technology begins to work, it will become easier for you to believe. Then a positive cycle, the opposite of a "vicious" cycle, begins. Before you know it you will be creating

Wherever I go, quality men immediately notice that I am a quality woman.

quality men at the market, the bank, the gym, the mall, everywhere you go!

Always Trust Yourself

An important final note: It is vital that you understand the difference between a belief and a gut instinct. If you see someone and you get that instinctive, intuitive "knowing" that this person is dangerous or bad, trust yourself. Do not second-guess that you might be creating that reality. Just get away from that person.

Fate, Destiny and Coincidence

Sometimes you tell the universe what to do, and sometimes it tells you what to do! When it does, listen. Let's say, for example, that you are on your way home from work one day, and you plan to stop at the market. You are daydreaming about finding Mr. Right and you bypass the turn onto the correct street, which causes you change your route. Then later you find out there was a terrible accident on the route you were originally going to take.

This alternative route just might cause you to end up stopping at a different store than you had originally planned. If you have been affirming that "people are all in a bad mood," you will likely end up at the market where everyone is unhappy. If you have been affirming the man of your dreams, you may find that your Prince Charming happens to be shopping there too. (Many things like this happen to me all the time.) This is the universe responding to our expectations, *so make sure you are "expecting" only the things that you really want to come true!*

Chapter 18
Once Bitten, Twice Shy

I'm not sure why we humans are wired this way, but it would be safe to say we are hard-wired when it comes to experience and expectation. I'm talking about our deductive reasoning turned against us—the way that our past shadows our present and how it affects the choices and decisions we make.

The human mind is not always logical in regard to the reason we give for why something went the way it did. Often we will blame the outcome of a particular situation on something that was not really the cause. It's the same mechanism that has us behead the bearer of bad news.

If what I just said has you thinking, "What the heck is she talking about?" that is understandable. The concept I am about to unfold is an illusive one. I will have to reveal it to you one step at a time. I promise that it will make sense to you soon. I also promise that it is relevant to attaining the love life you desire. So please bear with me.

We All Do This to Some Degree

Here is the story of a girl we will call Elizabeth. This brilliant young lady went to school for what seemed like decades to get the proper degree so that she would become qualified to do, and be able to get, a particular job.

Elizabeth worked her tushy off and therefore graduated at the top of her class. She then spent years climbing her way up the ladder of success. Then she put together an exquisite resume. Then she applied for that "Dream Job," a job which she is totally qualified to do, and perfectly suited for. So with great references to back her up, she goes for the interview, during which she is completely honest and herself in every way.

Lo and behold, Elizabeth gets the job! She goes home and calls all of her friends saying, "I knew I would get the job, because I was wearing my lucky underwear!" Freud probably has some great explanation for this completely irrational thinking! We all do this to one degree or another.

Let Me Put That Another Way

Has anything like this ever happened to you? You get into a car accident on the way to a specific location. Then the next time you head to that location, you think twice about going—as if it were the destination itself that caused the accident.

Or have you ever gotten sick after eating a particular food? Let's say it was after eating your favorite potato salad. Now you won't take the chance of eating it, even if you are craving it again. The fact that you ate it many times before without getting sick makes no difference to you. You don't even know which ingredient it was that made you sick. You figure that it was probably the mayonnaise in the potato salad that caused you to get sick. But you continue to gob the mayo onto your daily sandwich without a second thought. Now, does it make sense to deny yourself the pleasure of your favorite potato salad, while continuing to use mayonnaise?

Did you know that if you put a flea inside a jar and close the lid, the flea will try to jump out of the jar once and hit its entire body against the lid? You can now remove the lid, but the flea will never try jumping that high again. It will starve to death rather than risk that pain again. We humans have this same survival mechanism. Unfortunately, if we are unaware of it, this survival mechanism left to its own devices could lead to our demise.

We Are All a Little like Fleas

I see this kind of been-there,-done-that,-it-sucked,-so-I'm-not-gonna-do-it-again thinking holding women back in their love life all the time. So often I hear women discount almost every possibility that exists for meeting a PIP.

Here are some examples of what it sounds like: "I would never go out on a blind date again. I went on one once and it was a total nightmare!" Or, "Bars are a terrible place to meet men. I met a guy in a bar once and he only wanted me for one thing, and it wasn't my mind!" Or, "There is no way I would date a bookworm. I did once and he turned out to be a weirdo!" Or, "I dated an investments broker once and he was a control freak. I would never date a guy who works in that field again."

One bad experience and we discount an entire population or location. Could you imagine if we lived the rest of our lives this way? We would only have to stub our toe once getting out of bed and we might as well commit suicide. The problem isn't getting out of bed or

the bar or the profession. We just have to keep our eyes open and be aware in any situation. Mark Twain said it so well, "We should be careful to draw from an experience only the wisdom which is in it.

This kind of "*pre*-judgmental" thinking also clouds our view in terms of age, wealth, looks, race, religion, ethnicity and so on. Take a moment to see if you can think of any "entire populations" you have discounted.

Be Careful What You "Think" For

One of the most frequent and destructive examples of how this mindset messes with romance is the old "There are no good men in the city where I live!" This belief really creates a problem, since you are eliminating the "entire population" of men that you have access to. If you are at all resistant to what I am saying, then you should read very carefully now.

First of all, is it even at all possible or feasible that there are no good men in any one geographical area? Oh, I see, "All the good ones are taken, or gay!" Again, does that really make sense? *Have you even met every single man in the group you are excluding?* No, but you have already made a very destructive decision about every last one of them.

Secondly, what possible good could come of having this negative thought process? Now you are relating to every geographically desirable man, from a position of having already decided that he is "no good." Fat chance he has to make a good impression on you. Even worse, you are creating a horrible self-fulfilling prophecy for yourself. The same holds true for any other group you have excluded.

Have you ever thought that there are no good men in the area where you live? Have you discounted any other "entire populations"? Do you say any other all-inclusive negative things about all men?—including statements like "Men are dogs" or "Men are not attracted to women like me" or "I attract only the wrong men." Stop now and ask yourself, "Why would I have set up such a negative reality for myself?"

Untying Emotional Knots

If you came up with something that will make a positive impact on your current outlook, great! If not, it is important that you do figure out why you are sabotaging yourself in this way.

This is the first step to untying these emotional knots so you can open your mind and heart again. Think about when you are trying to untie an actual knot. Imagine a horrible knot in your shoelaces. If you begin to randomly pull on the laces, the knot is likely to become tighter. It is wiser to look closely and analyze how the laces are bound and carefully unbind them.

I will now illustrate several possibilities of how we may have come to make these decisions that do not work for us. You may be able to relate to one or more of them, possibly all or none of them. If you cannot relate to any of these, it is important to analyze your own particular "emotional knot" so that you can effectively untie it. If you just keep trying to have a relationship without untying it, you may end up tightening it, complicating it and/or adding to it.

A Road Well Traveled

Here is a path that I have seen many people take to get to this kind of negative mindset. See if you can relate. Look back and see if maybe there was a time when you experienced a series of unsatisfying attempts at romance. At that point you may have begun to think, "There must be something wrong with me." Ewww! Thinking that feels horrible. The only way to get around thinking that thought was to find another reason for your situation.

The next thought may have been something like "There must be something wrong with him!" Ahhh! That feels better. But if that was the sixth man in a row you'd said that about, it might have lost its power.

The next step is usually "There must be something wrong with men, all of them." I have known many women to get stuck there. They lump all men together by saying, "Men are all the same, no good!"

At times I have been tempted to get stuck there myself. I resist doing so because I know that if I did, I would become hopeless and then I would give up. If I give up, I know I will not ever love again. That is something I am not willing to give in to, so I refuse to get stuck in "Something is wrong with men."

We don't even want to go back to "Something is wrong with me." Right? So the next logical place to go from there is "There must be something wrong with 'IT,' the whole darn thing!" We might also say, "Men and women just cant be happy together" followed by some reason for that. Or, "I just can't be happy with a man because...."

Well, if that's true, again, that means love is a hopeless endeavor. We don't want to give in to that, so we better narrow it down. Finally we come to "There must be something wrong with 'here and now.'" This thought feels all right because a future "then and there" exists to keep us hopeful. In other words, we believe that there are men in some other time or place that we could have a good relationship with. This feels like the only safe mindset to take on! Of course, by believing this we have now subconsciously completely discounted every man who is in the "here and now."

The problem is that "the future never comes," in the literal. There is an undeniably true saying that perfectly illustrates this point. *"No matter where you go...there you are."* It's like the bar that has a sign that says "Free Beer Tomorrow!" They never really have to give you the free beer because at the time when you are there, it is never "tomorrow."

Love and War

Another possibility of how we came to negative mindsets about men as a whole has to do with another side of "human nature." It's the same part of our psyche that war makes sense to. I will illustrate what I am talking about by sharing a piece of history few people are aware of. I know how the war in the Middle East really started. Being of Syrian and Jewish descent (on my father's side), I represent both sides. My ancestors told me this story via internal communication.

The war between the Jews and the Palestinians originally had nothing to do with religion or land when it began. One day long ago, there was a Jew and a Palestinian who had a disagreement about something—it doesn't matter what. Both were passionate men from strong cultures and the debate became heated.

Before anyone realized what was happening, insults began to fly. Horrible insults about each other's families. The two even attacked the integrity of each other's mother. This could not be tolerated and a horrible fight ensued.

The fight did not stop until one was dead. It does not matter which one lived and which one died. The one-who-died's family became outraged. They cried, "A Jew" or "A Palestinian" (depending) "killed my brother."

The mourning family vowed to avenge their brother's death. They went out and killed a Jew, or a Palestinian. Though the one they killed was not the man who killed their brother, they felt justified—an eye for an eye, a life for a life.

Now this *new* dead man's family felt justified going out and finding one from the other group to kill. Again they killed someone who was not actually the one who killed their brother, just one from his group.

This vengeance-killing continued until every Jew and every Palestinian had a brother killed by the other. This is what all war, gang fighting and family feuds are really about. This is what is "worth dying for." And it all started with two people who nobody alive today even remembers. Two men who got hot under the collar and decided to fight to the death.

These men were not fighting about religion or territory. Their original fight didn't even have to do with their ethnic or cultural differences. It only became about that after the fact, for the family of the one who died.

What's the Difference

You see, when someone hurts us, we look to find the most obvious difference between them and us. Once we find that difference, we blame what happened on that difference. Suddenly anyone who bears that same difference is to blame. If someone of a different race, culture, religion, age group or sex does something bad to us, we blame all who are like them.

Let's say a particular type of person cuts us off in traffic. We will say, "All of those kind of people are terrible drivers." If someone from one of those groups cheats us out of our fair share, we think,

"Those people are cheaters."

Obviously, it is not all of the people in that group who did us wrong. There are rotten people and wonderful people in every group. We are "had" by our nature and can't help but lump people together based on what makes them different from us.

In many ways women and men have gone to war. We have all been hurt by someone of the opposite sex at some point in our life. Since the most obvious difference between them and us was our gender, we now conclude that "men" will hurt us. We actually begin to equate men and pain.

We look at all men, or particular types of men (those who are the same type as the one who hurt us before), as if they were the one who did that original damage. We mistrust the whole lot. We feel justified in doing what we need to do in order to protect ourselves. If we end up hurting one of them in protecting ourselves, we feel like "Hey, an eye for an eye." We begin to subconsciously see them all as the enemy. At the same time, we hope so deeply to find one we can trust with our love.

Bitten by Love

Another possibility of how we came to a negative mindset about certain types of men, or men in general, could be a survival mechanism turned against us. First I want to give you an example of how this particular mechanism works in our favor.

One day, a long time ago, a group of *Homo sapiens* were walking along when they came across a snake. They had never seen one before, so they did not know to be afraid. The snake bit one of the people and he died a horrible, painful death.

Those who saw what happened now knew that snakes are deadly. They now knew to be afraid and steer clear of snakes. They knew that if they came across a snake, they should go into "fight or flight" mode. This way of learning has worked well for our species, but it can really cause problems if we aren't aware of it. We must overcome this instinct when we see that it is doing us harm.

Many of us have been bitten by love, and are now shy of it. We see the possibility of love and go into "fight or flight" mode. For some of us, just laying eyes on a man who interests us can throw us into a "kill or be killed" instinct. This is not exactly beneficial in the pursuit of a healthy relationship.

Survival Can Be Painful

We might be led to setting up negative mindsets about men through another innate survival mechanism turned against us. Like the flea, we would rather die (never love) than take a chance of feeling that pain (a broken heart, betrayal, etc.) again.

First, an example of how this particular mechanism can work in our favor. At my hair salon I have a low-hanging decoration in a spot I walk past many times a day. When I first put it up, I hit my head on it about five times. *Ouch!!* Now, I just naturally duck every time and go under it. I don't even notice that it is there. (Which just goes to show that fleas learn faster than I do.)

When a particular action causes pain, we naturally discontinue, avoid or alter that action. This is a survival mechanism that works well to keep us from clunking our heads on low-hanging decorations. If, however, love has led to pain in the past, we may have made a subconscious decision to duck or avoid love at all costs. Our mind can be very creative and tricky in how it keeps us from risking pain.

Our Mind Has a Mind of Its Own

We are extraordinarily complicated beings. We all have conflicting thoughts at times. We are all familiar with the idea of a devil on one shoulder telling us to do one thing, and an angel on the other advising us to take a different route. So the idea that our mind has more than one motivation at a time is not outlandish.

I say that our mind has a mind of its own. Imagine that you have a separate being cohabiting in your head. I am not saying that you have multiple personalities like "Sybil"; instead, this is quite normal and healthy. This other "mind" is how we are able to play "devil's advocate" for ourselves. Most of the time it keeps us balanced. It helps us to weigh risk versus reward, selfishness versus selflessness, and all of those shades of gray.

Usually this head cohabitant is our friend, sort of like a "brain buddy." But sometimes even our closest friends, who want the best for us, can become overprotective. They may advise us to play it safe, even when it is not in our best interest in the long run. Really they just don't want to see us get hurt. Our mind can be very tricky in how it makes sure that we stay "safe." It would rather say "no" to the possibility of love because of some outside factor, than admit to us that it is saying "no" because it is committed to us not risking.

When you boil it down, a commitment to safety equals an unwillingness to love. Love is risky, that's a fact! Our mind knows that we would not let it get away with blocking us from ever loving. It knows that we would override those thoughts. Our mind is frightened that it would then have no way of protecting us from the possible pain that could ensue. So our mind makes up reason after logical reason for why we should not choose love. Believe me, if your mind is committed to preventing you from loving, it will not run out of reasons. Tricky, huh?

In order to find love we absolutely must undo any negative mindsets about men, love or relationships! We must use logic against our mind. We must realize that we are choosing to "not love" for the sole purpose of avoiding the possibility of pain. In doing so, we are hurting constantly. Life without the possibility of love is, in and of itself, painful. If we don't learn to manage our mind, no man will stand a chance with us and we won't stand a chance with love. But, how do we do this when the decision itself is subconscious?

The first step is becoming aware of it. You've now done that. Personally, I don't believe that you ALWAYS have to get down to the specific incident that first brought on the fear. Sometimes you can just make a conscious choice to now be open to love, EVEN THOUGH it is scary for you.

I am about to give you some techniques for overcoming fear. But you should know that just by knowing and understanding the things we have covered in this chapter you'll now start to notice when you are stuck in a trap. You will now naturally find yourself unwilling to give in to your mind. Instead you will *use* this new logic and push yourself to make a different choice.

Overriding Fear

Do not waste your time trying to make the fear go away. Just start allowing yourself to experience the feelings you are afraid of, even though they are scary. I highly recommend a book called *Feel the Fear and Do It Anyway* by Susan Jeffers, Ph.D. This book will give you the courage you need to get you past the self-defeating thought patterns that have kept you from having what you want.

Here is a great technique for overcoming fear: Say a positive statement over and over in your mind to counter these internal fears. I use the refrain from the old song, "Better to have lost in love, than never to have loved at all." This one works so well for me, because I am accepting that love *could* lead to pain, while affirming that if it does I will be okay, and that feeling love is worth feeling pain, if my fear of loss comes to fruition. I consciously choose to risk pain, because I would rather risk pain than never experience love.

Sometimes my fear can become so intense that I have to go for something on more of a gut level. When I feel so confronted by what may come that I become like a fish out of water (internally flopping around in complete panic), I say the following: "Everything is going to be all right. I will survive. I will THRIVE." You are welcome to use these if they work for you. If not, get to the core feeling that accompanies your fear and then find a statement that calms you. Say that statement over and over as often as you need to.

Such a Dive

Here is another great way to handle fear. Use this anytime you have decided to do something despite the fact that it is really scary. It's just like diving off of the high dive.

Imagine yourself standing at the foot of the high dive for the very first time. You look at the ladder that leads to the diving board and think, "*Yikes*, that looks scary!" Now, make a decision to climb the ladder anyway and deal with the fear when you get to the top. When you get to the top, you look at the end of the board and you think, "*Oyvey*, that is too scary!" Now make a decision that you will deal with the fear when you get to the edge of the board. When you get to the edge the board, don't think…JUMP!

By the time you hit the water, you will have dealt with your fear! Then you will either be clear that your fear was unfounded and you want to do it again, or you will know for sure that the high dive is not for you. Either way you will be proud of yourself and you will have overcome your fear!

The Light at the End of the Tunnel

The most important thing is to notice anytime that you are discounting an entire population. When you do, stop yourself. Tell yourself that it is not really true that everyone who is in the group you are disqualifying is the same way. Open your mind to all possibilities. Remind yourself of what you have just learned.

We must be diligent to undo all of the decisions we've made to discount entire populations of men. This does not mean that you ignore your gut feelings that warn you away from a particular man.

The healthiest balance occurs when we are both open to the possibility of meeting a great guy anywhere, and aware that any guy can turn out to be a jerk. It takes time to know a person's true character. It takes even more time to find out if that person and you are the right combination for each other.

Sometimes our deductive reasoning can work against us the other way around. We might think if we meet a guy at church or temple he must be a great guy. This of course is no truer than any of the other ways that we lump entire populations of men together.

Don't think you know if a guy is good for you or bad for you based on where you meet him or on any outside factor. If you trust blindly or mistrust blindly, you are likely to get yourself into trouble.

NO-GOOD DIRTY ROTTEN LOSER!!!

When you have a date or a relationship that doesn't work out, avoid the temptation to besmirch the guy. Don't call all of your friends and tell them what a low-life scum he was. When you do, you run the risk of starting up a new negative mindset—which can easily lead to disqualifying an entire population.

When a romance doesn't fly, we feel the need to blame someone. As we discussed before, we don't want to think that there is something wrong with us. So we have to find something wrong with them. We have seen that when we play the blame game, everyone loses! Because the next time we meet someone who resembles the one we are now blaming, we think, "No thank you! Been there, done that." Of course, just being male means they resemble him. See how it starts?

Instead, tell yourself and your friends that he just was not the right man for you. It is fine to analyze and explain in depth why he was not right for you. It is even good to vent, discuss, commiserate, even laugh about the specific things that made him not right for you. But unless he did something really horrible, dishonest, mean or hurtful, avoid the temptation of making him into a totally worthless, rotten, good-for-nothing subhuman. (Okay, maybe for just a few days.)

Final Note

If you try, but are unable to remove the blocks that keep you from allowing yourself to love, therapy may be the answer. I have never thought of myself as being mentally or emotionally unhealthy. Still I have benefited greatly from several forms of therapy, including traditional therapy, hypnosis therapy, Shakti healing and so forth. I have also learned tremendous amounts from self help books, tapes, seminars, workshops and so on. I am open to anything that cannot harm me and may lead me to a better understanding of myself or a more fulfilling life.

Chapter 19
I'm Psychic

I can foretell your future. But like all who soothsay, it depends entirely on the decisions you make and the "forks" you take. Most psychics will tell you that they can only see where you are going to end up if you stay on the path you are currently on. Most of us believe that we are the creators of our own destiny and that the actions we take determine our destination.

Why am I stating the obvious? It's because we seem to lose sight of this reality when it comes to romance. People are always saying things like, "If it is meant to be, it will happen"—as though they do not have any say in the end result, as if their actions have nothing to do with the outcome.

I believe in allowing things to happen as much as the next guy. But, what would happen if we took on this thought process about the rest of our lives? What if we said, "If I am meant to get to work today, it will happen"? We all know that if we want to actually make it to work, we have to take specific actions, like gassing up the car, getting in the car, turning the key, and so on. If we do not take these necessary actions, no matter what fate had in mind, we will not end up getting to work.

Now, if you get in the car and the car won't start when you turn the key, that is a different story. At that point I'll buy it, that you were fated to have a day off eating bon bons by the "boob tube."

Love Algebra

Romance is like anything else: You have to add action to fate to make things happen. Cupid's arrow is the variable. Even so, you must do your part. Fate and Cupid's combined effort won't stand a chance if you don't work with them. Here's the equation:

Fate + Cupid - Action on Your Part = No Love Result.

No Action = No Result

The point is, if you see someone that you like and you don't take any action, the end result will surely be no result. If you take an action, it could be the wrong action or the wrong guy and you still may not achieve the desired result. However, if you say the right thing to the right guy, now we're talking results.

It is important that you stop and realize that no action equals no result. With action, you may achieve the desired result. I always want to say, "You have nothing to lose." I guess it's more accurate to say, "It's the only way you can *gain.*" Yes, you still may lose; if you keep trying you will win some and lose some. If you don't try, you'll lose some and lose some.

Here is my prediction for your romantic future: If you never try or take action, you will not move forward. Yes, there are those rare situations when romance falls into your lap. But even then, you have to be open to it and respond—responding is still an action.

Knights in Shining Armor

I have heard women say, "If he really wants to be with me, he'll find a way." What do they think men are made of? Only men in the movies continuously keep coming back for more ego-battering "no's" in order to get that one special woman.

In the real world most men are as afraid of rejection as you and I, with these two possible exceptions: The first is the most insensitive breed of the species. If a man has no feelings, you can't hurt them. These are the cocky/pompous men who hit on every woman in sight. They are easy to spot by their tendency to use tired old cheesy lines. Another clue is that they don't *believe* "no" for an answer. I know I don't have to explain any further—if you've ever gotten the cheese-whiz treatment, you know it. *Yuck!*

The other kind of guy who will come back for "no" after "no" is the "only-want-what-I-can't-have" type. Keep in mind that if this guy finally does "find a way" and he "gets you," he won't want you anymore. If he only wants what he can't have, and he now "has you"...

Healthy men have a healthy fear. They are smart enough to walk away from someone who will reject them. Unfortunately, sometimes they are not smart enough to catch a subtle hint that you would *not* reject him.

Notice that the men you want are the ones who are most likely to need your encouragement. So many women say, "The only men who like me are creeps." It would probably be more accurate to say, "The only men who 'come on' to me are creeps." This is because quality men don't "come on" to women. If you maintain a "let them come to me" attitude, this is too much for a nice man to overcome. This does not mean that the nice men don't want you, it just means they won't push themselves (uninvited) onto you.

Please also keep in mind that men have also been hurt by women. Men are like fleas too. They are "had" by all of the same survival mechanisms and instincts that we are. They may also be so afraid of pain and rejection that they will avoid anything that may lead to that feeling. Just like us.

BAM!

That is why I recommend the anvil method (described in detail in the chapter "The Clincher!"). Basically, it's a matter of dropping a heavy enough hint that you like him, that he cannot miss it when it lands on his head. Doing so will enable him to get up the nerve to take a chance and ask you out.

No matter how clear you *think* you are making things, if you are not absolutely sure that he knows you *would* go out with him, keep hinting. Start out subtle and work your way to bold "anvil" measures.

Make Your Move

I often find myself coaching women who have been "jazzed" on a guy for months without doing anything about it. I advise them to take action. They'll say something like, "If he wants to be with me, he'll let me know; I am not the pushy type." I can't tell you how many men say the same thing about women they're crazy about. If nobody makes a move, no movement takes place.

Not to mention that many a man doesn't even notice a

woman until he gets the feeling that she likes him. Then all of a sudden he starts to see the light, and "stars." *Healthy, quality men like women who like them!*

Once upon a Time

I will now tell you the story of one woman who represents many. She is a hair client of mine—we will call her Carrie. She was completely *goo-goo* over this guy at work for the longest time, but just couldn't get up the nerve to give him a clear sign. We will call him Harry.

Then one day another woman walked in and scooped Harry up out of the singles pool, right in front of Carrie's nose. Carrie became so angry at this other woman, she proclaimed, "She was so pushy, so forward, she just walked in and started blatantly flirting with him. She practically asked him to ask her out!"

I tried to point out that maybe this behavior that Carrie deemed "pushy" is why that woman got Harry. She made it risk-free for him. Different than pushy, she didn't even ask him out. If a man is shy or sensitive, he will not want to chance rejection. Carrie had told me repeatedly that Harry was a sweet and gentle man, never pushy or overwhelming!

I finally got it through to Carrie that someone has to be the one to "push things forward." The next time she came in for a haircut she had a new boyfriend. She told me, "I thought about what you said, and what Harry's new girlfriend had said to Harry that day. The next time I came across a guy that I liked, I used her technique (the anvil method) on him and it worked. I feel like I should write her a thank-you!"

The moral of the story is, don't commit Harry Carrie! (Sorry, that was bad.) Actually there is a strong moral here. Fate led Carrie to something even better than Harry: the ability to meet and get a date with any Harry she may come across. That lesson is what was "meant to be."

He Likes Me, He Likes Me Not

As a final note to this chapter I want to tell you something that surprises people about me: Many of the men that I give my number to don't call.

Just recently I saw a sweet-looking lad at a billiards hall. Instantly, I surmised that he would be the type of guy who needed the anvil treatment. He seemed shy. I went up to him and started a conversation about pool playing. He appeared to be delighted. We talked, and he seemed as though he liked me. But I was not sure he was getting it, that I was interested in him.

He was not particularly handsome, but there was something about his energy I really liked. I looked pretty terrific that night, if I do say so myself. The look on his face seemed to me like he was thinking, "Wow, I can't believe she is talking to me!"

After about an hour, I had to go. I shook his hand and, as I expected, he did not ask for my number. Too shy? Maybe. So I said, "Aren't you going to ask me for my number?" He said, "I-um-er-um, YES!" He quickly and nervously tried to find a pen.

Why Ask Why?

He never called. Now, I could get all upset or hung up on why. But why? The fact that he did not call only proves one thing: He and I could not have worked out. No matter what the reason was that he didn't call, that would also be the reason why he and I wouldn't have worked out. Allow me to illustrate...

If this guy didn't call because he was too intimidated by me, then obviously a relationship would not have worked between us. Maybe he didn't call because he didn't like it that I was forward enough to offer my number. Well, if I hadn't he could not have called me anyway, since he wouldn't have had my number. And if he just didn't like me, then I wouldn't go out with him, because my first qualifier is that he has to like me.

Nerves of Steel (Not)

There was another guy I bombed out with recently. I had met him a few times before, and for some reason I felt such strong chemistry for this guy that every time I got around him I would get nervous. I would start to babble and stumble on my words. When I look back at what I said to him I think, "I probably wouldn't want to go out with me either."

Last time I saw him I decided to spill my guts. I told him that he made me nervous, and I actually thanked him for it (feeling "schoolgirl-nervous" is a rare and wonderful thing). I thought at least this way he might think, "Oh, that's why she seems so "wiggy" and flamboozled all the time." Maybe he would appreciate my predicament and be dazzled by my honesty. Maybe he would be so flattered that he would ask me out and I would have another chance to try to be my normal self. I kept thinking, "It seems like we would have a great time together if I could just relax."

He still hasn't asked me out (oh well). Again, I could get hung up on the rejection, but there is really no point. You see, if what I said did not endear me to him and make him want to go out with me, then we shouldn't go out. How do I know? I know because I was being who I really am and saying how I really felt. If he was gonna like me, he would have liked what I did and said.

On the other hand, some of my favorite stories about my favorite dates started by me stepping forward in these kinds of ways. Most of those men told me how attractive it was that I had the confidence to take the initiative and show that I was interested in them. For one reason or another, these men were not "The One" for me. They were, however, wonderful quality men that appreciated my boldness. Bottom line: Letting men know where I stand has won me many winners and lost me only losing propositions.

Throwing Things at Men

At the risk of being redundant, I want to drive home this very important point once again in this chapter. Many women are very concerned and will ask, "Won't I appear desperate or needy if I throw myself at men the way you are suggesting?" You will only come off as desperate if you really are. If you feel desperate, that is just a sign that you should work on your confidence level.

If you come from a place of knowing and liking who you are, you can show that you like a man without appearing desperate. There is nothing more attractive to a man than a woman who likes herself showing interest in him.

Besides, I am not suggesting that you throw yourself at men. You throw a big heavy hint at him, one that just says that you are interested in getting to know him better. Your job is to try for him, without becoming attached to "him" as the outcome. If you are able to achieve this mindset you will be amazed, not only with how successful you become with men, but with how calm and easygoing you feel about the whole issue.

For the Record

As a final note to taking action in your love life: I am a firm believer in using every resource available to you. I am an advocate of being set up by friends, dating services, singles groups, personal ads, matchmakers, you name it. If you use any of these options the trick is to *use* them!

I often ask women if they have tried any of these and they will say, "Yeah, I signed up, but nothing has come of it." I ask them to tell me what *has* happened and they say, "Well I haven't gone there or taken any action."

On the other hand I know many women who are now living happily ever after who used a dating service, matchmaker or singles group to find their Mr. Right. These women stuck with it and really used the service they joined. These resources are a particularly good idea if you are at all shy. And the best thing about it is that you know that every guy there is single and looking.

Chapter 20
What If He Still Does Not Ask
(Or, How to Deal with Rejection)

What if he still does not ask, says no, or quickly turns and runs in the other direction? Wait, don't panic. Let's look at some possibilities for his reaction, or lack thereof. Maybe he has a girlfriend/wife, or he could be gay. He could have an old war injury that makes him unable to perform. It is possible that he is incapable of having a relationship due to his own emotional baggage or warped psychology. Or (Heaven forbid) your (and my) worst nightmare, it could be that he just does not dig us.

Please resist the urge to feed this book to your paper shredder, and read on, because finding out that a guy does not like us is a *good* thing. No, I have not lost my last marble (yet). Believe it or not, I actually have an ironclad argument for why this is a good thing.

Powerful Concept

It is so important for all of us to realize this single concept. If a guy does not like us, that fact, in and of itself, disqualifies him as a good partner for us. After years of putting myself on the line, I have achieved an incredibly healthy and wise perspective on handling rejection. If you want to adopt it, I will tell you that it requires a lot of effort and a strong will. But, if you can psych yourself into this mindset, you will be able to avoid an incredible amount of pain and fear of rejection.

I look at it this way: I am five feet nine inches tall with brown eyes, dark hair and a sizeable nose. The color foundation I wear is called "Beyond Pale." I am quite skinny, nicknamed "Bones," and I look nothing like Dr. McCoy from *Star Trek*. I have legs practically to my neck that are actually quite shapely, if I do say so myself.

If a guy is looking for a cute little tan blonde with a cute little nose that goes with her cute little butt and pretty, innocent blue eyes, I am simply not going to be his cup of tea, *period.* Now is blonde hair better than brown? Is a cute butt more important than long legs? Is a cute little nose really better than my big old honker?

NO. Beauty is *truly* in the eye of the beholder. It's a question of taste, like chocolate or vanilla. If a guy is looking for the cute little blonde with her tight little butt, then he *will* reject me. However, if he likes tall brunettes with long legs, I am his *dream come true!!* I am clear that I want to be with someone who would choose the latter, and if a guy wants the former, that in and of itself disqualifies him for me.

The same holds true on a more personal level. I am a strong, bold, extroverted woman. If a guy is looking for a shy, timid or quiet girl, he is not going to like me, NO MATTER WHAT, and that's good! In fact, I am glad we found out now and didn't even start a relationship because he would then set out on a mission to change me, which really sucks.

You're the Interviewer

If you can truly psych yourself into this mindset, you will find yourself able to be quite bold because now you're no longer trying to be liked. You're now interviewing to see if he qualifies for you, based on his likes...no risk! No desperation!! If he likes you, you're glad. If he doesn't, you're *still* glad.

It's not always easy to hold on to this thought process when you're in the situation, but like everything else in life, the more you practice, the better you get. It's like a muscle you're strengthening—one you weren't even aware you had before. The more you use it, the stronger you will become. Soon you won't even get sore anymore!

The Question Answers Itself

Keep in mind that no matter why a relationship with a particular fellow does not begin, it would not have worked out between you for the very same reason. What I'm trying to say is difficult to explain, so allow me to illustrate.

If a guy is a commitment-phobe and therefore cannot make a date, then his phobic tendencies would also make a relationship with him impossible. Say he is too busy, or your schedules clash and therefore you cannot seem to get together. Then he is too busy to get into relationship. Realize now that your schedules would be a constant source of contention, and would eventually cause you to break up.

Let's say a guy is G.U.D. (Geographically Un-Desirable), and he is unwilling to overcome the obstacles necessary to get you two together. Then he does not feel strongly enough about you, or passionate enough about romance, to overcome the obstacles that

APPLICA ON FOR A
DATE W H SUSIE
1. How do you like Susie?
Explain
ke animals?
2. Do
commitment
3. Are
phobi

would come up in a relationship.

Maybe the problem that keeps you from getting together with a particular PIP is that the chemistry just isn't there for him, though it may be like gangbusters for you. Then that inequity is the same problem that would break the two of you up later.

Say you do something that a guy does not like and he won't talk to you about it. Then his unwillingness to communicate would be the eventual undoing of your romance. It's just like if you have a conflict with a PIP, and the two of you cannot resolve it, so you never end up dating. It is this inability to resolve conflicts that would lead to the eventual demise of any relationship between the two of you. It never matters what the actual conflict was. It only matters that the two of you are not able to resolve your conflicts.

No matter which way you slice it, if there is any reason why you and a PIP don't get together, that is also the precise reason why it would not work out between the two of you in the long run. This mindset allows you to rid yourself of the old "If Only" plague and makes it possible for you to move on to the next opportunity.

Cure for the "If Only" Bug

Sometimes we are blocked from the love life we desire because we are sick with the "If Only" disease over an "old flame." It is hard to move on to a new relationship if we haven't resolved a past relationship. The above thought process works for getting over any ex-sweetheart, as well as a current "hopeful contender."

It does not matter what caused the breakup with an ex. It's the fact that the two of you were unable to work it out that matters. In other words, if there is any problem you couldn't resolve, then the problem is that the two of you are not able to resolve your problems.

It also doesn't matter why you couldn't resolve your problems. For instance, if you couldn't resolve them because he would not try or he gave up, then his flaw is the *reason* why the two of you couldn't resolve your problems. Can you see that this flaw of his was a fatal flaw and would not change over time? So if you hadn't broken up for the reason that you did, when you did, you would have broken up soon over something else. *If you end up in a relationship with a fatally flawed man, then the relationship is also fatally flawed.*

Here is a great quote: "You don't marry the person you marry because you think you won't have problems with them. You marry them because *they* are the person you want to have your problems *with.*"

If a guy does something that is unacceptable to you, then he is not an acceptable choice (or the right man) for you. The same holds true the other way around. If he cannot accept something you do, you are not right for each other.

My advice is to beat your "If Only" thoughts into submission with your logic. Note: The beatings begin only after you have sufficiently mourned the loss. Never suppress your emotions. They must all be felt and processed. Use the logic I have just given you to overcome the leftover regret and constant questioning of yourself.

It's a Produce Market

We've all heard the saying, "It's a meat market!" This is a negative statement that has men unfairly passing judgment on women. I say, "It's a produce market!" The way I have it framed is a healthy way to feel good about judging and being judged.

For instance, let's say I'm an apple and I only like oranges. In that case, finding an orange is only half the battle. Then I have to find out if the orange I found likes apples. If he does not, then I am not "right for him." This does not mean that there is something wrong with me, only that I am wrong for him.

The same holds true the other way around. Let's say a nice juicy peach comes along who likes apples, and therefore he likes me. Even though he may be the ripest, most succulent peach in the market, it doesn't matter to me, because I want an orange. There is nothing wrong with him, he's just wrong for me.

Once I do find that orange who is looking for an apple like me, I may take a big juicy bite and love it. However, I may find out later that oranges are too acidic for me and end up giving me an upset stomach. Now that I have found out that oranges cause me pain, I may become open to that peach. Or maybe I want to try a banana?

In other words, if you find that you want someone who does not want you, don't take that personally! Finding the one you like is only half the battle. That fruit has to be looking for the particular kind of fruit you are also. Then you begin to find out if the two of you even taste good together. Remember: *When someone does not want you, that never means there's something wrong with you.*

Low-Hanging Fruit

In life and in relationships, just as in picking fruit from a tree, it is best to go for that which is hanging low. If you are selling ice, why target the Eskimos? If your living is made providing your customers with frozen water, it would be better to display your wares to thirsty Saharans. In other words, look for those who are looking for what you've got.

There is no reason to get out a ladder and climb to the top of a tree to get that one piece of fruit at the top, when there are lovely juicy kumquats within your reach. In other words, you usually don't have to work really hard to get the man who is right for you, interested in you.

Al Dente

Here is one more food analogy and then you may want to take a break and get something to eat. A healthy and painless way to deal with rejection while finding the right relationship is to think about pasta. Do you know how you check to see if pasta is ready? You take a strand out of the pot and throw it against the wall. If it sticks, it's ready. If it doesn't stick to the wall, you don't feel bad about it. There's no sense of rejection, or fear that the pasta will never get done. You just throw it back in the pot (assuming it never touched the floor), keep cooking and remain patient. You know that it's worth it to wait a little longer for the pasta dish to be "just right."

The equivalent of taking a man out of the pot and throwing him against the wall would be to pull him out of the singles pool and go out on a date with him. If he doesn't stick (isn't what you want), throw him back. No need to feel bad about it. No reason to feel rejected or worry that you will never find "The One." You know that it's worth it to wait a little longer for the mate that is "just right" for you. My advice is to be patient—keep cooking and keep looking!

Chapter 21
The Problem with Games!

Some People Call Them *"Rules"*

There is a grave danger in playing games with romance. Early game playing is responsible for a large percentage of later unhappiness and disappointment in relationships. These disappointments often lead to breakups and disillusioned broken hearts on both people's part. The sad thing is, usually neither person can figure out what went wrong.

It is important to clarify exactly what I do and do not mean when I say "games."

A person may pretend to be different than how he or she really is, or pretend to feel differently than he or she really feels. If this is done for the direct purpose of getting a person to like us, or to keep a person interested in us, then we are playing games.

The Rules is a book that teaches women how to get a man to marry them by playing rotten deceptive games. The only time the authors' advice is not a game is when you really are the way it is suggesting you pretend to be. For instance, they suggest that you never talk to a man for long on the phone (they tell you to actually set a timer). If you are a person who really doesn't like long phone conversations, then that would not be playing a game for you.

The word "manipulation" gets a bad rap, though not all manipulations are bad or games. Telling a person they look good when they are visibly not at their best is not exactly being honest. However, sometimes a person is in a situation where they are unable to do anything about it. In this case, your response is a manipulation whose intention is to give the person confidence at a time when they need it. If someone says or does something stupid, and you say, "It's not stupid to me," then yes, you did not express your true feelings. But it was for the sake of sparing theirs.

Saying something for the sole purpose of getting a conversation started or getting a guy to ask you out would not be a "game." No, this is different. This is a strategy designed to create an opportunity to get to know each other better. If you're not sure whether you are playing games, manipulating or strategizing, ask yourself: What is the intended outcome of my manipulation? Would it benefit me only, or him, or both of us? Also ask yourself if you are pretending to be someone that you are not.

Examples of games are anything from playing "hard to get" to suppressing how you really feel, for the purpose of making someone want you. For instance, purposely not calling a man or showing him how interested you are, so that he will feel insecure and chase you, is a game. Spending the entire date asking him questions about himself because "men love to talk about themselves" is also a game. Not expressing anger or not asking for what you want because "men like to feel that they are in control," would also qualify as a game. Pumping up a man's ego by either laughing at jokes you really find offensive, or playing dumb so that he feels smart, would also be considered games. I think you're catching my drift.

The Trick's on You

Now, don't get me wrong. These are all quite effective tricks for getting certain kinds of men to like you. Yes, it's true, these games do work on many men. There is no doubt about that. The problem I have with these "tricks" (and it's a big problem) is that when you're done, it's not *you* that the guy likes. It's the person that you pretended to be. Do you really think that you can keep up this persona indefinitely? Do you really want to?!

For instance, if you're playing the aloof "hard to get" game, eventually you will want to show your partner that you like him. Especially if the end result you're hoping for is a lifetime partner. What happens when he *"gets"* (i.e., marries) you? Not to mention the question: Is a man who only wants or values what he can't have, a healthy person or a suitable choice for a partner?

Do you want to spend the rest of your life playing dumb, hearing only about his life, while he never asks about yours? Or listening to endless offensive jokes, and so on? What do you think is going to happen when you suddenly, one day, become who you really are?

Now you're in love with him. You basically have two choices: You could go on pretending to be someone you're not for the rest of your life (that sounds like a happy existence), or, when you do decide to "be yourself," you get the ax then and there. Or worse yet, you stay together and spend the rest of your lives making each other miserable because you are not *"really"* what he "signed up for," nor what he wanted.

What Kind of Fish Do You Catch with *That* Kind of Bait?

If we set out to play a game or pretend to be different than how we really are, in order to get a man, we must ask ourselves: What kind of man would be attracted to the type of woman I am pretending to be?

For instance, let's take a closer look at the psychology of men who like aloof women. These men only want what they can't have. They have an unconscious equation that says, "If she likes me, there must be something wrong with her!" Groucho Marx said, "I wouldn't join a club that would have me as a member." A man who is attracted by aloof women clearly has some stuff to work out in the area of self-worth.

On the other hand, a man who would be attracted to a woman who only asks about him and never talks about herself probably has the opposite problem. He's most likely narcissistic. A man who likes a woman who plays dumb or never asks for what she wants is probably a bit of a control freak. None of the men I've described are someone that I would want to spend the rest of my life with. Would you?

Bad Acting

This does not mean that you should now start acting opposite to any of the ways we have just talked about. You should not ACT at all. I know women who are naturally aloof. They, being who they are, tend to attract men who are extremely independent and would hate to feel crowded in a relationship. They are right for each other!

I, on the other hand, am not at all naturally aloof. If I played it that way in the beginning, I would attract a man who was turned on by that trait. BAD MOVE! Because later, when I eventually could not fake it any longer, we would end up in a tug-of-war over who I am.

The question of whether or not a man and a woman are right for each other continuously answers itself! Here's an example of what I mean. From the very beginning, if I want to call a guy, I do. If that turns him off, and he therefore loses interest in me, that is *perfect*. He should be with a woman who naturally doesn't want to call.

Conversely, I should be with a guy who likes it when a woman calls.

The point is not to become "*easy* to get." In fact, if you follow the advice in this book, you will probably become *truly* hard to get (different from aloof). What I mean is, when we know how valuable we really are, we do not choose to give ourselves away to just anyone. We take our time to get to know a man and see if he is worthy of our love. When we become more confident, we become more discerning. We are then *truly* difficult to pin down (hard to get).

They Can Smell It

Part of the problem when we play games is that whenever we are not truly being ourselves, the other person can feel that something is "off." For instance, say you are totally into a man you've met. You can't wait to talk to him. But a friend gave you some version of that old useless advice, "A man needs to feel that he is chasing a woman. He'll think you're desperate and not like you if you call him." So you use every ounce of discipline and strength in your body to keep yourself from calling him.

When he does call, you try hard to act unexcited, so that you won't sound desperate. Since you're having to focus on keeping up this "take it or leave it" attitude, you can't fully be yourself. Consequently, he is less able to make a connection with you, though he doesn't know why. He's more likely to be turned off by the inability to connect with you than if you had just been your real self in the first place.

In other words, if you're playing games, a man will feel it and dislike you for not being genuine. Believe me, they can smell it. If you're feeling desperate: Instead of concentrating on not *looking* desperate, work on not *being* desperate. Do this by working on your confidence level. Then you will not *be* desperate, but not necessarily aloof either. Be as available and interested as you really are. Work on truly *feeling* only as available and interested as is healthy for you.

When I call a man I like, I don't even allow myself to go into the thought process of "Am I calling too soon, or too much?" I am quite natural and confident about it. That's why it comes off like genuine interest—not at all clingy or desperate. The men I'm interested in really like it when a woman is interested in them, and is willing to show it! See how it works? Be yourself, and get liked by a man who likes women like you. The most common compliment I get is some version of "It's great to be with a woman like you, one who is real and not putting on any airs."

I'll Show You Later

Sometimes we are tempted to just temporarily try to appear different than we are, so we don't turn a PIP off before he gets a chance to know us. There are a few circumstances where I would not be against this. For instance, you don't have to go out of your way to tell a man details about your life that may initially be hard for him to swallow. However, if he asks you about something you would rather not explain, I believe you must either "take the Fifth" or tell the truth. No matter how bad your "detail" is, starting your relationship with dishonesty is worse! When it comes to your personality, it is best to let it all hang out.

A favorite client of mine—we will call her Catherine—once asked my advice. Catherine is a very powerful and successful independent woman with a brilliant mind, a strong will and a bank account to match. Needless to say, she is not the "damsel in distress" type. Don't get me wrong, she is all woman, a stunningly beautiful totally feminine flower. So you think "she's got it all!" Right? Believe it or not, she and many women like her often have more difficulties getting dates than those of us who may feel somewhat less blessed. Why? Men feel intimidated by them. If you fall into this category, don't worry. We've got you covered later in the chapter "Open Sesame."

Catherine asked me, "Felicia, should I pretend I don't have it all so together in the beginning? Should I act like I need a man more than I really do, in the traditional ways? Should I make them think I'm weaker, dumber or less independent than I really am, until they get to know me better and start to care for me?"

My answer was NO, NO, and NO! First off, if you are pretending to be something you are not, he cannot actually get to know YOU better. Second, what good is it to start liking each other when it's not "the real you" he is liking or relating to, only to find out later that you're not compatible anyway. Now it hurts to say goodbye!

The third reason is the most important to realize. The man who is strong and self-assured enough to be able to respect Catherine's strengths, as opposed to feeling intimidated by them, is a guy who would not settle for less. So if Catherine is busy acting different than how she really is, the man who would love her as she is, will not even notice her. And if he does, he won't realize that he has found what he has been looking for.

The more unique you are, the more important it is that you absolutely be yourself. If you are *not* being yourself when that (also unique) man passes by you, he could miss you! Always remember this: *The right man for you will love you most for what is most unique about you.*

Like It or Not

Based on this "be yourself and attract men who like women like you" philosophy, I never shut up. I naturally talk a lot, and want to be with a man who likes that quality in a woman. Yes, there are men who like that!! One of the best compliments I was ever given was that my verbose nature made me a great date. He said, "I never have to worry about the conversation lagging, or if we will have a fun date, or how I will entertain you." These were fears that this particular gentleman had. Several have said things along the line of, "I love to listen to you talk. I never know what you're going to come up with next!" There have also been men who did not exactly appreciate my verbal abundance. Okay, I admit it, there have been plenty that wanted to get out the duct tape.

Should I act like a mute in the beginning so I won't turn off a man who believes that "women should be seen and not heard," and then maybe he would fall in love with other aspects of me? Can you see that if I were to be successful in that endeavor, it would only lead to a torturous future?—for him, wishing I would shut my mouth, and for me, feeling his constant *attempt* (yeah, right!) at suppressing me.

It is much better for me to be with a man who loves it that I am bubbling over with things to tell him! The only mistake is to turn someone on or off by being different than who we are. If you are being you, and someone does not want you because of it, then that person is simply wrong for you. It really is all perfect, though it may not feel that way in the moment. In the long run, when you do find the man that is truly right for you, you will look back and say, "Not ending up with that other guy was *perfect.*"

Worst of All

Which brings me to the greatest tragedy that playing games can create. Say I meet a guy that I really like, and I take the aloof or "hard to get" approach. As it turns out, this guy can't stand aloof women. Now, by pretending to be a way that I am not, I've turned off and ruined any possibility of a relationship with a guy I've come across that would have liked me just the way I am. You can apply this tragedy to any of the games I have mentioned, and the many I have not.

He Loves Me, He Loves NOT ME

Finally, let's say you play a game and you and the guy end up in love. Now you will always wonder, "Did he really fall in love with *me*, or was it the person I pretended to be? And is he still in love with *her*, or is it really me now?"

One bright and beautiful woman I know told me, "I did *The Rules* on my boyfriend and it really worked!" I thought, "I bet this guy would have fallen head over heels in love with this wonderful, intelligent, kind, witty, beautiful woman no matter what!" Now, she is forever robbed of that knowledge. Sad.

I-Yam What I-Yam

I know it may be difficult at times to resist the notion that we need to be different than how we really are. I, too, am sometimes had by the thought, "I wish I were different from the way that I am." This thought is one that may never go away completely. I combat it with my Popeye mantra: "I am what I am!" I say it to myself over and over.

I try to prevent myself from even attempting to change myself into being what someone else wants me to be. I combat this tendency with the logic that I could not keep up any fake persona for long anyway. Besides, I know that you can't please everyone. If I changed to be what one person wants me to be, then I would displease those who like me the way I am. No, it is futile to try to be perfect, or to have everyone like me.

SPINACH
ACFernandez

In my healthier moments, I also realize that I like and love myself the way I am. I do not wish to change my innate personality. I'll keep me as I am even if someone I feel strong affections for would like me better some other way. I have a poem that helps me to keep myself grounded in this reality. It was written by an incredible artist/poet who happens to be my cousin.

Don't lose yourself in the hope of love,
It's advice I give myself.

Next time I'll take that stranger,
and put her on the shelf.

I like the real me
so why wouldn't he?

I know now, I must take this vow:
All that is important to me will remain so,
no more sacrifices or repressing the ego.

Of course I will accept differences and compromise,
love will happen through communication,
NOT HIDDEN LIES!

—By The Totally Fabulous Joy Kirschenbaum

Section V
How to Be a
"Quality Man Magnet"

aisle 2
canned goods
cereal
sauces
sugar

Chapter 22
The Key to Being Attractive

Nothing makes a woman more attractive to quality men than—what? No, it's not a big "set-o-hooters"! It's CONFIDENCE!! Confidence, however, can be intimidating if it is not carefully combined with approachability. This delicate balance is the key to being noticed and liked. It is "The Key to Being Attractive."

In this chapter and the next, we will analyze and dissect "confidence." Then we will spend an entire chapter on "approachability." We will look closely at every detail of the anatomy of each of these qualities. When we are through, we will be able to manifest these two attributes simultaneously within ourselves, at will. This will make us so attractive to healthy, quality men that we will act as a *magnet* for them.

In becoming confident and approachable, we become attractive to everyone. This includes friends, employers, people who serve us, and those we serve. Everywhere we go, life just becomes more fun. We suddenly find ourselves feeling great about interacting with everyone, including strangers.

What Is the Meaning of This?

First off, let's talk about exactly what confidence is. I always like to start by checking with Webster in these matters. Here is what the "big boy" has to say on the subject. There are two basic meanings:

The first definition of confidence is: "An assurance of mind or firm belief in the trustworthiness of another, or in the truth or reality of fact; trust; reliance." I am *confident* in your ability to understand what this means.

The second definition is: "Reliance on one's own abilities, fortune, or circumstances; belief in one's own competency, self-reliance." The first definition seems easier to accomplish. Most of us find it easier to have faith in other people's abilities than in our own.

The "little" Webster has a one-word definition: "Sure." This definition seems the most poetic to me. SURE; certain; without doubt; without fear, without hesitation. I think we get the gist of what good old Webster has to say on the subject.

Everyone's an Expert

I also interviewed a few of my favorite wise people on the subject. I asked them, "If you had to describe confidence to an alien, one who understood the English language and had some understanding of human nature, what would you say?"

I put this question to my most valued associate in my hair business, Cyndi. I have great respect for Cyndi's ability to know who she is, and to like herself as she is. She is excellent at creating healthy boundaries. I am often impressed with her ability to negotiate a terrific deal for herself. She is able to do this because she knows her own value well.

Cyndi says, "To me, confidence is the ability to trust in your own intuition. Your decisions and standards do not have to be right in someone else's eyes or right for them. When you are confident, you are open to others' opinions but not swayed by their judgments. It's all about self-respect."

My friend Chelsea, who is one of the most compassionate, non-judgmental people I know, says, "Well, little alien, true confidence comes from total self-acceptance. It's feeling good enough about yourself that you are not afraid to take on new challenges. It's also the ability to re-try old challenges, even if at first you did not succeed."

I asked my mom who, like myself, battles to maintain her confidence, though we have both come a long, long way. She says, "Confidence is what makes you feel that you will be able to handle a situation well. It is an aura you exude that makes others feel that you are capable also. It is strength and energy."

Rhoda, who is an incredibly successful attorney and entrepreneur and a mentor of mine, says, "Confidence is the knowledge that you can achieve anything you desire if you are willing to do what it takes." Rhoda is 64 and proud of it. She has always been a groundbreaking, rainmaking go-getter. I could literally write a book about her achievements.

I Think, Therefore I Am

Here is how I would describe confidence: "It's knowing yourself well and believing that you hold a high value. It's being proud of yourself and maintaining a high opinion of yourself. This sense of self cannot be shaken by other people's opinions of you. Your opinion of your own value does not change if you make a mistake or fail at something. Confidence is accepting yourself as a whole and complete, perfect being. Your flaws are a part of your unique perfection; that is what acceptance means." Note: acceptance does not mean you stop working to improve yourself. It means you don't dislike yourself or judge yourself harshly for your flaws.

The Comparison Price

Here are some things that are often confused with confidence: being conceited, cocky, pompous, stuck-up, or always right. The difference is that confident people know who they are and feel great about it, but don't believe they are better than someone else. There is no judgment in confidence. Your good feelings about yourself stand on their own.

People who are conceited or stuck-up are definitely comparing themselves to others, and thinking, "I am better than they are." Stop for a minute and ask yourself honestly if you have a tendency to compare yourself to others. If you find that you do, don't get mad at yourself for it, because this behavior really comes from fear.

Being conceited or stuck-up is actually the opposite of being confident. Conceited people are actually very UN-sure of themselves. So unsure that they need to compare themselves to someone else who comes out "not as good." This is the only way they can feel better about themselves.

If you think that you may fit into this category, do not beat yourself up for comparing, because that will only lead you to doing it more. Instead, give yourself a loving and accepting hug. Remind yourself that you are not God. Therefore, it is not your job to be flawless or to judge others. Make a new commitment to accept both yourself and others.

No-Win Situation

I am not suggesting that you make this change because you are a bad person for comparing yourself to others. I am recommending that you change because comparing yourself to others is always self-defeating.

Let me explain. When you compare yourself to others, you may begin to feel great about yourself because you see that you are better in a particular way than somebody else. The moment that you do, someone else will come along who is better still. Then you end up feeling like *"doody."* For example, you may be the fastest runner on earth, but there will still be somebody else who can outdistance you.

Thinking that you are better than someone else is a false high, and when you come down to earth, you hit the ground hard! It is best to just keep your feet on the ground to begin with.

Honey or Vinegar

Conceit acts as a repellant to healthy, quality people. However, it can attract people who have low self-esteem. Insecure people may feel that the only way they can "be somebody" is by attaching themselves to your identity. It's similar to the way many teenagers with low self-esteem will try hard to become friends with the "in crowd." They may do this regardless of whether they like or respect these popular people, and even if these people are not nice to them.

If, when you compare yourself to others, you tend to come out "not as good," this stance is less offensive to others, but is still unhealthy. This is the other side of low self-esteem and will attract people who are conceited. The conceited person will use your feeling inferior to them as a way of feeling better about themselves. In this scenario you are the one attaching yourself to their identity so that you can feel like "a somebody." Neither position is healthy or good for anyone.

Healthy friendships add dimension, perspective and joy to our lives, not an identity. We are all responsible for maintaining our own identity, independently. We know we are headed in an unhealthy direction when we look to anyone else to provide us with an identity.

Really, it is best to just give up the entire "comparison" thought process. When we do, we find life much more entertaining and way less stressful. If we don't give up comparing, we will never be able to achieve true confidence.

Instead of comparing, ask yourself if you are you doing your "personal best." If you are, discipline yourself to be proud of yourself for that. Avoid even asking yourself if someone else would have, or could have, done better. Commit yourself to being happy with being great at certain things, fair at some, and lousy at others. Decide that you are who you are, and accept yourself fully.

If You're Green, You're Growin'; If You're Ripe, You're Dyin'

Accepting yourself does not mean that you stop working on yourself. It means that you accept that you are a work in progress. We all want to improve ourselves. This is healthy, as long as we don't beat ourselves up for what we have not yet accomplished. Anytime you are beating yourself up, you are not moving forward toward your goals. Self-anger is always counterproductive.

If you do find that you are beating yourself up, it can be incredibly difficult to stop because it's a vicious cycle. I have been working on this one for a long time. I have come to the point where the thing I spend the most time beating myself up for, is beating myself up. Try getting out of that one.

Counter Active

The way to stop beating yourself up is the same way we dealt with negative self-fulfilling prophecies. Remember our pickle/cheesecake analogy? You cannot not think what you think, but you can choose to think another thought as well. The trick is, anytime you have a negative (self beating) thought you must counter it with three positives. The positives have to be specific and must directly counter the negative.

Here's an example of beating yourself up countered by three specific positives:

Negative: "I'm such a wimp. I had an opportunity to talk to a PIP and I blew it! I am so stupid. I never know what to say."

Three specifically counteractive positives:

- "I am strong and brave and growing stronger and braver every day!"
- "I am smart and creative and am becoming more outgoing every day!"
- "I am learning from my experiences. I am smart enough to look back at a situation that did not go the way I wanted it to, and figure out what I could have done differently. I am a quick learner and will do great the next time!"

Notice how I specifically countered the negative aspects of what I had said before? Even if you think this won't work, what do you have to lose by trying it? I ask that you try it for at least one month before you discount it. You must keep it up long enough for your subconscious to get used to this new opinion of yourself.

Unacceptable

In my seminars when I talk about self-acceptance, someone will inevitably bring to my attention that this acceptance thing can be taken too far. They say that they "know people who do things that are totally without integrity and then they just accept it." This usually stirs up a big commotion in the room. In case you are thinking the same thing, I will handle accepting the unacceptable right now.

There are some things that are unacceptable. Self-acceptance does not give us the right to hurt people, lie, cheat or steal. If you see that you are behaving in a way that is hurtful to someone, or is not in accord with your sense of integrity, stop immediately!

Some people, do something awful and then just accept it. They'll say, "Oh well, what's done is done, nothing I can do about it now." Others, after realizing they have done something awful will begin to feel guilty. They may beat themselves up for some time. Then, when they feel they have been miserable long enough and "taken their punishment," they try to forgive themselves. This is totally ineffective, because they cannot truly forgive themselves. This also does nothing to undo the damage they have done, or help the person they have hurt. The only way to accept something like this is to do absolutely everything you can to remedy the situation and make amends.

Handling Mistakes

If you ever find yourself in this guilty position (and who hasn't?), here are the "Four Steps for Handling Mistakes," also called the four A's. I learned these when I was a volunteer for the Youth at Risk Program. This is an organization designed to empower inner-city youths to realize their full potential. Some of these kids had already done some horrible (hard-to-accept) things in their short lives. It was imperative for them (as it is for us) to internally attain a clean slate. This way they could gain confidence and start fresh.

Go to the person that you have hurt and do the following:

1. Acknowledge your action.
2. Accept, or take responsibility for your action.
3. Apologize.
4. Amend, or do whatever you can to clean up the mess.

This will enable you to really forgive yourself, and then you will be able to fully restore your confidence level.

There are times, however, when spilling your guts and telling on yourself are the wrong things to do. In order to decide if that is the case, ask yourself the following questions: "Does the person I have wronged stand to be hurt worse if I do not tell them?" For instance, could they find out elsewhere in some more painful way that you lied?

Or could their not knowing the truth put them in harm's way? For instance, if you cheated on your partner and the sex you had was not safe, then you must tell.

"Would telling the person I wronged benefit them in some way? Can I make amends?" Sometimes we tell a person something just to relieve our guilty conscience, though it only causes them pain. This is selfish. On the other hand, if we have stolen or lied about something that has cost the other person, we can tell them and then make up for it.

How do you restore your confidence in a situation where you realize it's better to keep your mouth shut? It is difficult, but not impossible. First, you must do your best to understand why you did what you did. This is the only way you can be sure that you can stop yourself from doing it again. Then, make a commitment to never do it again. Finally, you must find some way to make universal, or secret, amends.

Here are some examples: If you took drugs while on the job, you could volunteer at a drug abuse hot line. If you stole money from a friend, you could deposit the same amount (plus interest) in their jacket pocket when they aren't looking. Depending on what you did, you may have to get very creative to figure out how to make your silent, or universal, amends.

I cannot overstate how important it is to rebuild your sense of your own integrity. It is vital to achieving a high level of confidence. Feeling guilty does not relieve you of the guilt. Taking action and making amends will restore your faith in yourself.

Chapter 23
The Lock-Pick Set

Okay, now we have a clear picture of what confidence is, what it is not, and what it can do for us. We are aware of some of the blocks and pitfalls that will keep us from attaining confidence and how to overcome them. But how do we achieve confidence in the first place? I've got some great stuff on this one.

First, Know Thyself

You know *you* better than anyone. I know that sounds obvious, but I want you to really think about it. You know yourself from the inside out. You know every thought you think. You know what your true intentions are. When a friend tells you that she got a huge raise and you say, "Congratulations!" Only you know whether or not (down deep inside), you are really happy for her, or if you are thinking, "*'Glitch!'* She didn't deserve a raise, I hate her!"

Keep in mind that we are all human and having some of these kinds of thoughts is just in our nature. If you let them run rampant, however, they will stand in the way of your confidence. If you look at yourself and see something you don't like, do what you can to change it.

Can't Bear to Look

Not only do you know the dark side of yourself, you also know how wonderful you are. This positive side, believe it or not, is often more difficult for us to look at than the "icky" side is. Why is this?

From a very early age it has been drilled into all of our heads that it is somehow wrong, bad and conceited to think highly of ourselves. Society, the media, and our own trusted parents and family have told us that we SHOULD NOT "toot our own horn." We SHOULD NOT "be full of ourselves." We SHOULD be humble, unassuming and self-effacing.

First I want to say, if I am not supposed to be full of myself, just exactly who am I supposed to be full of?! And what is the fun in having your own horn if you're not allowed to toot it every once in a while?!

Next, I want to inform you of what our old friend Webster has to say about the word "humble." The synonyms are: humiliate, mortify, lower and disgrace. The synonyms of "efface," as in "self-efface," are: erase, obliterate, cancel, expunge, blot out and destroy.

This is what we are SUPPOSED to do to ourselves? Doesn't that make you mad? No wonder we have a slightly ill society. Is it any wonder that low self-esteem is so prevalent? "Humble" and "efface" are violent words. Though we are not consciously aware of their definition, subconsciously we are.

It is important for us to understand exactly what we are up against internally. What stands between confidence and ourselves are all of these negative messages that were drilled into our head in childhood. These messages were deposited in our psyches in our formative stages. They went in before we had any logic with which to filter them. For just one moment, suspend those beliefs that have been forced on you, and take on this one instead: "It is good for me, and everyone around me, for me to feel FANTASTIC about myself."

You're Soaking in It

You may have a hard time getting that message in past all of the old stuff still stuck in your noggin. If so, it is a good idea to meditate on the concept. When I say meditate, I mean to kind of soak your brain in it. To do this, repeat the following sentence to yourself, in your head and out loud, over and over until you begin to accept it.

> *"It is good for me, and everyone around me, for me to feel FANTASTIC about myself."*

Now I am going to describe an incredibly powerful exercise, one of only two in this book. Do this exercise every day for a week. If it has really started to take effect, you can do it every other day for a few weeks. When it becomes second nature, you can just use it formally anytime you feel your confidence begin to wane. To do this exercise you will need blank paper and a pen. Please wait until you have them in hand to continue reading.

I'm Fantastic!

Exercise Your Way to Health

Three inches from the top of the paper, write the following in capital letters:

"WHAT'S SOOOOOO GREAT ABOUT ME!!!!"

Underline it and put quotation marks around it. Then draw the top half of a sun above what you just wrote. (You are drawing the sun because you are about to see the light!)

Now number "1" through "5" down the page. Then fill in five great things about you. Write any five things about yourself that you like. For some of you, this will be easy. For others it will be incredibly difficult. The more difficult this is for you to do, the more you need this exercise.

For those of you who are having a hard time coming up with great things about yourself, I will give you some ideas. If any of them fit for you, please steal them. I already know some great things about you just from the fact that you are reading this book. For instance, you are open-minded and smart. You are also proactive! Here are some others that may fit: Are you kind, fun, honest, or a good friend? Now you come up with some of your own. Put down this book until you get to five.

Now go ahead and number to "10." Fill those in. I'll throw a few more out there for you to steal if they fit for you. Are you creative, nice, or sensitive? Write down absolutely anything you like about yourself. Remember, the harder this is for you, the more you need it. You must not give up!

Now number through "20," and fill them in. Do as many as you can, but at least get to 20, before moving on! When you do this each day, I suggest starting with a fresh piece of paper. It is fine to repeat the same things you wrote the day before, but think of them newly each time. No copying from yesterday's paper! You will see that each day it gets easier and easier to do.

Are You Getting Your RDA?

I am constantly hearing people say that they suffer from "low self-esteem." They talk about it as if it were a condition like diabetes—as if it's something they just have to live with. Low self-esteem is more like a vitamin deficiency than anything else. We are each responsible every day to see that we receive our "Recommended Daily Allowance" of self-esteem vitamins (RDA—you know, just like on the back of a cereal box).

Nutrition Facts

Serving Size: 20 Affirmations per day

Recommended servings: Twice daily

Amount per serving	RDA*
Confidence	100%
Approachibility	100%
Self-Esteem	100%
Strength	100%
Courage	100%
Heart	100%
Total Success Ratio	100%

* RDA = U.S. Recommended Daily Allowances

Also note that your parents cannot give you a low self-esteem. They could have when you were a small child, but, they can't now. This is evident by the fact that you are the only one who can give yourself a high self-esteem now. Your parents may not have taught you good self-esteem habits, but it's up to you now to build your own good habits.

The more aware you become of how wonderful you are, the more everyone else will seem to notice it also. If you do your "self-esteem-ups" (exercises) every day you won't believe the difference it makes in the way all people, but especially men, see you. You will literally become irresistible to quality men.

Stinkin' Thinkin'

Remember how we handled negative self-fulfilling prophesies and "beating ourselves up"? This is also the way to handle negative thoughts about yourself. You must counteract the negative thought with three specific positives.

Negative thought: "I'm ugly!"

Here are three positives that specifically counteract that "ugly" thought:

- "I am pretty."
- "I exude beauty from inside and out!"
- "I have a warm smile that goes with my beautiful eyes!"

Know This

If you've read all of this and think it is a good idea but you don't actually do it, it will not make a difference in your life. Likewise, if you do it once or twice and then stop, it will not make a *big* difference. These techniques and exercises will raise your confidence level only if you do them—and keep doing them.

However, if you do take this advice and regularly write down your positive qualities and continuously counter any negative thoughts, you will have miraculous results. I promise. In fact, if you take only the advice in this chapter and do nothing else differently, you will still be amazed at how much more you will "meet and attract quality men."

This is like brushing your teeth, you do that so you can keep a full set of teeth. The by product or side effect is a pretty smile. Doing your affirmations and focusing on only positive thoughts is like "mental hygiene." You do it so that you keep your confidence up. The by product or side effect is that you become incredibly attractive to men (and everyone else).

I am a loving, caring,
unique, charming,
intelligent, special person.

Magnifying *Mirror Mirror on the Wall...*

While I'm on the subject of beauty, we women have a terrible self-destructive habit of hyper-focusing on every flaw (no matter how small). I know I said I don't believe in rules. But these are the exception:

Rule #1. Focus on your best points. I mean any spot on your body that you like at all—and completely ignore any flaws. Take me, for example. I hate my elbows with a passion. I have absolutely no rear end. And my nose has a strong point, which is not exactly a strong point. I used to focus on these things, and then others did too. I also have beautiful eyes, great legs and gorgeous earlobes. Now I focus on those parts, and the great thing is, so do others.

Rule #2. No insulting yourself!! You must always say positive things about yourself. Always avoid insulting yourself whether inside your head or out loud. This means you never say, "I'm so stupid!" or "What a klutz I am!" *No saying bad things about yourself EVER!*

How are you going to build your confidence if you are saying bad things about yourself to yourself? Know that what you say about yourself goes right into your head, without being filtered. Your mind thinks, "I wouldn't lie to me."

Rule #3. ***Always avoid*** **pointing out a flaw of yours to a PIP!!!** If he does not notice, why alert him? Even if he does, talking about it doesn't make it any better!

I had a client once who I knew for quite some time. I had never noticed that she had a bunch of wobbly skin on the underside of her upper arms—that is, until one day she made a point of telling and showing me. Now every time I see her, I notice it. Just don't point out your own flaws. DON'T DO IT!

Be sure to read about how to psych yourself up for a date or for any situation where you might get an opportunity to meet PIPs, in the chapter entitled "Self-Fulfilling Prophecies."

Chapter 24
Open Sesame

This chapter discusses the second half of the key to being attractive. We will now nail down *approachability.* This attribute is vital to giving a man the courage to talk to you and to ask you out. If you are not approachable, men will not even want to try to talk to you.

The information in this chapter will also work with the rest of the world. You can use the advice given here to help you feel great about meeting any new person. We can all use more friends and contacts. I'm talking about the ability to network with anyone anywhere, a skill that is extremely valuable for everyone.

Active Ingredient

Approachability is a necessary ingredient for any woman to attract men. It is especially important for women who are very pretty or powerful, or who seem to have it all together. Even though these are wonderful qualities, they can be very intimidating to men.

Men may assume that other men you consider "better" than them are asking you out all the time. They may feel that the competition is just too stiff, and therefore not even try for you. Furthermore, we all become more nervous around PIPs who really get our motors running.

The Missing Link

If you have even the tiniest inkling that you might fall into the category of very pretty, "together" or powerful, you most likely *do.* I believe this to be true because we are all our own worst critic. This chapter may provide you with the missing link to your success.

Here is the story of a hair client who took my seminar. We will call her Dana. Dana definitely fit into this category, though she was unaware of it. She had been having a real problem attracting anything but egotistical, controlling, high-powered men. They were very handsome and successful, but they weren't what she wanted.

Dana told me that after attending my seminar, nice men started to come out of the woodwork in droves. When I asked her what she had changed in terms of her behavior, she said the main thing was that now she was smiling at everyone. She told me that she was now regularly using all of the information about how to be approachable.

Shy?

If you are shy, your shyness may cause you to appear unapproachable. Many times when people feel shy, they don't look at, smile at or speak to others. NEVER UNDERESTIMATE THE POWER OF A SMILE! People may interpret silence as a negative vibe. Therefore, you must force yourself to at least smile. If you have to look away right after the smile, that's okay. You just have to give people some sign that you do not dislike them and that you are friendly.

How Do You Feel?

Approachability comes from compassion and sympathy for how the other person feels. The first step to understanding how others feel when meeting you is to put yourself in their shoes. Stop and think about how you feel down deep inside when you meet a new person.

Most everyone feels some degree of discomfort when meeting new people. There are those who are painfully shy, while others feel only a slight twinge. In order to understand exactly where this uncomfortable feeling is coming from, imagine yourself in a situation where you would feel that specific discomfort to an extreme. A scenario that works for most people would be walking alone into a party where you don't know a soul. Another would be the first day of a new job. Really put yourself there. Can you feel the discomfort? Can you pinpoint the feeling? If so, what are you specifically afraid of? Can you pinpoint the reason for the feeling, or the underlying thought that accompanies it?

Like-Minded

No matter what you came up with, I'll lay odds ten to one that if you boil it down far enough you will come to some version of a "fear of not being liked." The most popular responses are, "I'm afraid I won't have anyone to talk to" or "I'm not sure what will be expected of me" or "I'm not sure what to expect" and so forth. All of these responses, and probably any you came up with can be boiled down to the fear of not being liked.

If you were sure that people would like you, you'd feel sure you would find someone to talk to. You wouldn't worry about their expectations being met—or your own, for that matter. Some may say, as I once did, "I don't care what people think of me." This is just our ego's tricky way of shielding us from the deep-down fear.

Whether or not you see yourself as someone who is afraid of not being liked, I have a request. For the sake of this discussion, I ask that you assume that just about everyone is afraid of not being liked. Also note that this fear is intensified when we are interested in someone romantically.

Foolproof

I will now share with you a foolproof way of overcoming this fear. This method will also ensure that everywhere you go, just about everyone you meet will like you. It comes from the realization that everyone else is afraid of *the exact same thing!*

You may already know this. But do you really think about it? Are you very aware of it in the moment when you are meeting a new person? Most people are so busy feeling their own fear that they are (in that moment) completely unaware of the other person's fear.

As soon as you become acutely aware that whenever you are meeting new people they are scared to death that you won't like them, you begin to feel a strong sympathy, even empathy, for them. You naturally find yourself trying to make the other person feel at ease. You begin to strive to let them know that they don't have to worry. You become so concerned about their feelings that you forget to be afraid.

That's the Trick

Like them first. Sound simple? The concept is. But you and I both know that if you go around saying, "I like you!" to people you have just met, they will think you are weird or crazy, or both. So, you don't say it like that. It's more in the way you carry yourself and your body language.

Showing any interest in a person says, "I like you." Asking questions and listening to what people have to say also works. Even just paying attention to them will get the job done. Any compliment expresses affection and approval. I am not saying that you go around brown-nosing people. Everyone has something about them that warrants a compliment. You may have to find out more about them to see what it is.

Desperately Seeking Reality

I want to go over a few things from other chapters and illustrate how they relate to approachability. The first is about the fear of looking desperate or needy. Here is an important truth to realize: You will only seem desperate or needy if you *actually* are.

Desperation and neediness are manifestations of an emotional attachment to being liked. They have nothing to do with liking someone. We can like someone and yet be unattached to their liking us—meaning that we feel confident enough to like them and if they do not like us, that is perfectly all right with us. This stance is the most attractive to others. Can you see that this stance is utterly confident and not at all desperate?

I am constantly hearing men and women talk about who called who, and debating how long one should wait to call a PIP so as not to seem desperate. This thought process is so silly. Where did it even come from? I guess it originated in saving face, and ended up a strategy to manipulate others.

This game never works. Let's say you want to call a guy but do not want to appear desperate. So you don't. If that guy likes you based on the fact that you didn't call, he is liking you for a game you were playing and not for the way you really are.

This game can also backfire. I have known many men and women who decided against going out with a PIP based on the fact that the PIP did not show enough interest. I always wonder if the PIP didn't call because he or she was playing this game.

Put Your Cards on the Table

I advise calling when, and as often as, you feel like calling. I also recommend showing interest and affection exactly as much as you feel it. If that is too much or too little for the other person, this is just a sign that the two of you are incompatible in this regard. At least if things do not move forward, it was for an authentic reason. The same goes for showing people that you like them.

A commitment to save face is a decision to lose by default. In poker this would be the equivalent of folding, just so we don't have to face the (possible) "awful truth" of what cards the other person is holding—when for all we know we could have won, if we were willing to risk.

If you sometimes feel "attached" to another person liking you, this is totally normal. If you feel that way constantly, this is just a sign that you need to work on your confidence level.

Confidence is simply a skill, a muscle to be built up. Use the effective exercise for strengthening this muscle that is found in the chapter "The Lock-Pick Set." Likewise, if you don't have a lot of friends, this does not mean that you are unlikable. It only means that you need to work on your "creating and keeping friends" skills. And if you don't have as many dates as you'd like, that too is just a skill to be developed and strengthened.

It's My Party

Here is a great mindset to adopt in order to put all of this advice into action:

> *Think of the world as a party and you are the host. It is your job to make sure that everyone feels welcome and is having a good time.*

People feel comfortable when they feel liked. Here is a technique I have been known to use in group situations. I will go up to someone I've never met, who is standing alone, and introduce myself. They then introduce themselves to me in kind. Then I introduce myself to someone else, and then introduce the two of them.

They now feel better because they know someone, and I get the credit for introducing them. All of a sudden I'm Ms. Popularity. Mind you, I am not doing it for the credit or the popularity. I am doing it because I can't stand to see anyone standing lonely and frightened all alone with no one to talk to.

Whether they really feel this way or not, my interpretation of their feelings puts me in a different mindset—one that will get me past my own fears and enable me to take an action that works for everyone. If you take on the belief that everyone you meet is afraid that you won't like them, then you will naturally start to come up with your own methods that work for you.

Chapter 25
Men's Shoes, Second Floor...Ladies First!

A man can see a woman walking in a pair of high-heeled shoes and think, "Boy, it looks like it would be difficult to balance, and painful to walk around in those things." He can be sympathetic, but unless he is into cross-dressing, he cannot be empathetic. No, a man cannot experience for himself your foot pain. He does not know if your heel hurts worse than the ball of your foot, or how much it hurts. He does not know which is more challenging in heels, uphill or down.

A man may not support you in just the right way as he helps you out of the car. This is because he does not understand which of the laws of physics is most likely to be holding you back with those torture devices on your feet. He only knows that high heels look great on women and he wants you to wear them. He may also second-guess any feelings of sympathy he has for you. He sees many other women walking around in shoes like that with no apparent problem.

We women think we know that it is scary to ask someone out on a date. We think we are empathetic to what a man feels when he asks a woman out. We believe we understand the challenges he faces when he has to open his mouth and lay his head on the chopping block. But unless we have actually taken a walk around the block in those shoes, we do not really know how it actually feels.

We don't know which hurts worse, the "I just want to be friends" type of "no," or the "I'm already seeing someone." Just as, there are subtle difficulties in wearing high heels that one would never think of unless they tried walking in a pair. You can be sure that if you have never asked someone out on a date, you are not aware of all of the specific difficulties and challenges involved. You can sympathize, but unless you've done it yourself, you cannot empathize with what you are asking a man to do.

Your Mission

There are only two exercises prescribed in this book, and here comes the scary one. Hold on to your hats, ladies, because you may feel a sudden breeze. Some of you may even be blown away. Your mission, should you choose to accept it, is to ask at least one man out. I really recommend two, but see how just one grabs you, and go from there.

If you have asked men out before, look back to when you did it. Did you point-blank ask a guy out on a date? Or was it kind of a vague invitation? I'm talking about something where the guy had to give a yes or no answer—where if he said "yes," you and he were going out on a date, not just "getting together."

Resist the Urge

At this point, many of you may feel a sudden urge to put this book down for a while. WAIT! Before you do, I want you to know that you may feel so confronted by what you have just read, that you may not be able to pick the book back up. If that is the case, you have my permission to just read this chapter and not do the exercise. *Please be aware* that this experiential part is probably the most valuable part of this book. And believe it or not, carrying out this exercise will actually do more toward making Master Dating easy for you than the entire rest of the book combined.

Warm Up, and Stretch

In this exercise, as in yoga, you should only stretch yourself a little bit further than is uncomfortable. If you have never even come close to asking a man out before, it's okay to start with a vague invitation. Eventually, though, you should get to the "point-blank question" (after all, that is what we are asking men to do). If you've only done the "vague invitation" thing before, then you should do the "point-blank" thing now.

There are those of you who have asked some men out, and just get a little nervous at the moment of truth. You will need to be creative and come up with just the right exercise for you. Find a way to stretch yourself, some way to purposely open yourself to a possible rejection that would feel devastating—something that makes your heart race and your tummy turn upside-down.

I know that sounds sadistic on my part and masochistic on yours. You must understand that this is what most men will have to go through if they are to ask you out. The point of all of this is to put yourself in the man's shoes.

A small percentage of you have asked many men out and have no problem in doing so. It will be the hardest for you to find a way to experience how men feel when confronted with the opportunity to ask a woman out. This is because in the same situation you would not feel the same way. Since nobody knows you better than you, you are the only one who can come up with your exercise. Your job is to find some way for you to experience that feeling of "rejection terror." You must always remember, it is easier for *you* to ask someone out than it is for most men.

Once you have personally felt what a man will feel if he is to ask you out, you will automatically become empathetic to his plight. You will really *know* exactly what would hold a man back, what might keep him from approaching you or asking you for a date.

Your having had this personal experience of facing the specific obstacles that men face when asking a woman out will enable you to remove those obstacles for the man. After you do this exercise you will find that your part (all of the other stuff I recommend in this book) comes naturally and easily for you.

My Scary Story

I came upon this exercise accidentally. In my "research" I had heard over and over that men love it when women ask them out. I was skeptical. But I decided to give it a try anyway. Keep in mind that I always thought the reason I was good at getting dates was because I was so sympathetic to how hard it must be for a man to ask a woman out.

I had no clue what I was in for. I am a gutsy woman. I karaoke for fun. I sing full-out, and I'm not being humble when I say I don't sing well. I have also performed with my own material in front of crowds of up to two thousand people.

I once dared someone to dare me to go up to this insane man who was standing naked on Hollywood Boulevard and ask him if he knew what time it was. It was so funny. The guy got mad at me for tricking him into looking at his wrist. It was apparent he was not wearing a watch. What I am trying to point out is that it takes a lot to frighten me!

Eenie Meenie Meinie Moe

I carefully picked who I would ask out. He was a guy I did not know. Therefore, I wouldn't have to deal with any future embarrassment if things didn't go the way I wanted. I picked someone I was interested in enough that if he said yes, I would be glad to go on a date with him. But I wasn't so into him that I would be crushed if he said no. I thought, "Keep the stakes low, this will be a breeze."

I decided to ask this guy I had met at a N.A.W.B.O. (National Association of Women Business Owners) meeting. I didn't know much about him. I thought the fact that he was at a women's networking group spoke highly of him.

I deliberated long and hard about what I would say. I noticed that figuring out what to say was much more challenging than I had expected. Finally, I felt that I was ready. I took a deep breath and picked up the phone.

The Moment of Truth

Well let me tell you, every time I dialed the phone my entire body would revolt. I literally shook from head to toe. Condensation began to accumulate on all surfaces of my body. I could not seem to breathe properly. My belly was doing flip-flops, and my brain was short-circuiting. My tongue was apparently tied in a knot.

I only had this guy's business card. So I had to call him at work. When the receptionist answered, I could barely get the words "May I speak to David Smith, please?" out of my mouth (the name has been changed to protect the innocent). I thought to myself, "Oh my God, this is only the receptionist I'm talking to. What is going to happen if I actually get this guy on the phone?"

It took several calls before I got him in person. During those endless moments on hold, I found myself praying, "Please, if he says no, let him tell me it's because he has a girlfriend!" I couldn't care less if that was truly the case! That was the moment that I decided from now on, if I turn a guy down I'll use "I'm taken" as the reason. That is the only way for a person to not feel horrible about being told "no."

Finally, he was on the phone. All of the previously described physical manifestations of terror became even more extreme. But I had no choice. I had to go through with it. I was committed! I had practiced what I would say many, many times. I was so nervous that even the moment I got off the phone, I couldn't remember if I said my "spiel" the way I had planned or not.

No Fair

What had I planned on saying, you ask? Okay, I'll tell you, but I feel like it's cheating, since part of what's so difficult is to figure out what to say. An important thing to note is that we often expect men to think of these things on the spot. Men usually do not get time to think, let alone practice what to say.

This was my "spiel": "Hi David, my name is Felicia. I met you the other day at the N.A.W.B.O. meeting. I'm not sure if you remember me—I'm the hairdresser who asked the speaker the question about...You seemed like a nice guy, and I wanted to know if you would like to join me sometime for a cup of 'joe,' a glass of wine or a bite to eat?"

It was probably only seconds before he responded, though it felt like eons. Finally he said, "Wow, I'm so flattered, but I kind of have a girlfriend." I thought, *"Thank you, thank you, THANK YOU!!!"*

Whew!

Since then I have asked two other men out. I was surprised that the whole thing did not become any easier. Both of these men said yes. The dates had an uncomfortable feeling to them. I'm not sure if it was their discomfort or mine. Maybe both of us felt uncomfortable with our roles.

My Findings

In terms of research, my findings were as follows: While I do believe that a man loves it when a woman asks him out, I'm not convinced that he loves the woman who did the asking.

In other words, I can see that being asked out flatters a man and he loves that feeling. So yes, "men love it when women ask them out." However, my experience was that asking him did not necessarily make him like me. I decided I like it better when men ask me out.

The big lesson for me was how incredibly difficult it was to get up the nerve to ask someone out. Having more nerve than almost anyone I know, I found myself in awe of every man who has ever gotten up the nerve to ask any woman out. And I was asking out guys I didn't even really like that much, or care if they said yes. I can't imagine how hard it is when you are really attached to the result.

After those experiences, I naturally became *empathetic* to what I used to be *sympathetic* to. From that empathy, I started to really Master Date. My success instantly tripled!

Now that I truly understood the man's dilemma, I could greatly minimize his risk and fear. I learned how to "grease the slide" for men to ask me out. I can now empower a man to ask me out in just minutes, and it is not even difficult to do. Once you complete this exercise, you will naturally start to be able to do this too!

No Way Around It

If you think that just by reading this chapter and imagining how difficult it would be to ask someone out, you will become empathetic, *you are wrong!* Even getting close to asking a man out will NOT get the job done.

In order for us to really know what we are expecting men to do, we must actually walk the distance in their loafers. This is the only way for us to personally understand what would prevent a man from asking us out, so that we can remove those blocks.

Remember, I am not suggesting that you ask a guy out as a means to an end of getting a date. No, you are asking him out only so that you can experience what it is like to do the asking. I recommend that you choose a guy that you can take or leave. If you are really stuck on a guy, use the other techniques in this book to get him to ask *you* out. This way, you don't take a chance of making either of you feel uncomfortable by confusing your roles.

Chapter 26
The Clincher!

This chapter is the reason you went out and spent your hard-earned money to buy this book. If you use the advice given here on any man that is even slightly romantically interested in you, you will get a date with him within minutes. Fine print: (Offer is subject to the density of some members of the male persuasion, and your ability to communicate between the lines.)

All of the chapters up to now were designed to help you get yourself into a situation where you will use the advice in this chapter. They were also meant to prepare and empower you to be able to get up the nerve and confidence to do the very important step I am about to reveal.

Here's the Trick:

You must find a way to let him know, without actually saying it, that if he asked you out, you would say "yes!"

Seem simple? It is, and it isn't, because you'll have to be somewhat subtle, and at the same time you must make him feel *sure* that you would say "yes." Yet, you want to reserve the actual asking for him.

There are many ways to do this, and timing is everything. You don't always get a clear sign that the moment is right for "The Clincher." You are looking for any signal that the PIP likes you. I mean any sign at all, no matter how small. Then you must commit yourself. No chickening out. Take a deep breath, and you are ready to proceed.

Every situation is different, so you have to be looking for your opportunity. If the PIP is someone you won't end up making contact with again unless you make a point of doing so, then get creative and do so.

The Anvil Method

Once you are in a conversation with a PIP it can be as easy as, "Hey, what are you gonna do this weekend?" If he tells you about something good, you might say, "Gee, that sounds like fun. I wish I had something like that planned for *my* weekend."

If he doesn't get it yet, try something like, "Tell me more about your plans." As he continues, you make comments like, "I *love* to do that kind of stuff." To you, it will feel like you are hitting him over the head with an anvil. However, from his perspective, you could just be talking about the weekend.

If he starts giving you details about the activity you were talking about, so that you could go and do it yourself sometime, you will have to get bolder. I'd say, with a big smile, "Well, it wouldn't be any fun unless I was doing it with someone fun like you, anyway." My experience is that most men (if they are interested in you) will get it, and ask you to join them. Or they will try to make another date with you.

Delayed Reaction

If at this point he does not ask (assuming he is single), he may be dense or gay or just not interested in you. The other possibility is that he is a bit slow on the uptake. So if you use "The Clincher" on a PIP and you don't walk away with a date, hold your reaction. Don't get your feelings hurt, or make any decisions yet. Try to remain open-minded to a delayed reaction on his part.

Most people will feel a sense of anger toward any person they perceive to have rejected them. This is not good for you or him, or for any possible future between the two of you. Many times I have had to talk friends and clients down from this anger reaction.

Here is the story of one woman who represents many. We will call her Heather. Heather had been *gonzo* over this guy Joe who worked in her building. They had seen each other many times and even spoken a few times. Heather thought that he might be showing signs that he liked her. One time, Joe asked Heather to exchange business cards with him, in the elevator (how daring). I agreed that this was a good sign and recommended that she use "The Clincher" on him. She did so and called me the next day.

"Felicia, I did what you said. I went for it. Yesterday, I felt like I practically begged Joe to ask me out. He just stood there and acted like he didn't get it. Now I don't think he even liked me to begin with. If he's too dense to see that we could have a great time together, I don't want him anyway. Then today, he calls me to see if I want to go to lunch with him. Forget him and his mixed signals. Hot then cold, and now hot again. I just told him I already had plans, in the most monotone voice that I could muster."

Then I had to work hard to convince Heather that it just took

Joe a while to figure the whole thing out. Now that she's turned him down for lunch, he's thinking, "Gosh, I thought I figured out that she wanted to go out with me! Guess I was all wrong." Now he feels rejected also. Of course, this makes it even more difficult for him to get up the nerve to ask again.

Dear Gabby

I am not just making up the guy's reaction. Over the years, many men have called me in situations similar to Joe and Heather's. They want to get my opinion about whether or not the girl likes them. They give me the whole story in four-part harmony. Even thirdhand, it is so clear that the woman involved was hinting that she liked him. Often, I can't believe that the guy is not suffering from a mondo-sized headache from being hit over the head with that anvil.

Finally I convince him that the girl was trying to get him to ask her out. I tell him it was a mistake to not clearly show her right then that he liked her. The next day, I get the call. He says, "See, you were all wrong! I called her today to ask her to lunch and she cold flat turned me down!"

All Tied Up

In order to keep yourself out of this kind of tangled mess, follow these instructions carefully. Here is what you do if you use "The Clincher" on a guy and he does not ask you out. First read the chapter "What If He Still Does Not Ask (or, How to Deal with Rejection)" so you won't feel bad inside. Then remember to keep your mind open for a while to see if he figures it out (better late than never).

Also note that the more afraid of rejection he is, the more sensitive he is. The more unaware he is that a woman is coming on to him, the more unassuming he is. Then again, there is such a thing as too sensitive, and too dense—and you can get to a certain level of humility and you cross over into unhealthy. So take it all as information—not about you, but about him and any potential relationship between the two of you.

Heather took my advice again and called Joe to ask him to lunch the next day. She said, "Sorry I was so blunt on the phone yesterday. I was having a bad day. It had nothing to do with you. Would you like to do lunch some other day this week?" He said yes.

They started going out and Heather called me to say (my favorite words), "You were right! Joe and I were talking and I asked him why he didn't ask me out that time when I was hinting. He said, "I did, as soon as I figured it out."

Meanwhile, Back at the Ranch....

Now back to our original scenario. Remember, we were asking a PIP about what he is going to do this weekend. What if he says "nothing much," or tells you about something awful he has to do? Then you could say something like, "I'm trying to figure out something fun to do this weekend. Everyone I've called so far already has plans."

This, in and of itself, doesn't get the job done, but it is a great setup. It gives him the opportunity to invite you to do something. He could also recommend ideas of things he likes to do.

For instance, he might say something like, "You should go to the beach and go boogie-boarding." Then you could ask, "Oh, do you like to boogie-board? I've always wanted to learn how to do that. If only I had someone to teach me." Then wait—he should get the idea. Again, if he doesn't make his move, assume it is thick-headedness and not a rejection. Keep trying to let him know, "If you ask me, I'll say 'yes.'"

It is not uncommon to come across men who are clueless enough to start explaining how to do the activity they are suggesting. I will say something like, "I learn best by doing. Maybe you would teach me how sometime." They will usually bite that bait.

Wait Not, Want Not!

If he says he will personally teach you how to do the activity, SET A TIME—RIGHT THEN AND THERE! Don't wait. That is the final ingredient to "The Clincher." You *must* set a date. Here is how you do it: You say, "When would be good for you?" Try it with me now. Come on, say it out loud: "When would be good for you?" I am making such a big deal about this because it is the part we are all most likely to forget in the excitement of the moment.

Here is a cherry for on top (assuming your intuition is telling you that he does like you in a romantic sense). When everything is all set, finish it off by saying, "I'll be looking forward to our date!" If that does not feel comfortable for you, say it another way. The idea is to mention that *"this is a date."* If you set a date for Friday night, you could say, "Friday night is my favorite time to go out on a date." Doing this will save you much afterthought about whether he thinks of this as a romantic thing or "just a friend" thing. He also gets to bypass this confusion.

Who's Strange?

What about when you've just met someone? How do you use "The Clincher" to empower a stranger to ask you out? Be sure you read "Master Date Safely" in the front of this book, and the "Final Safety Warning" in the back. Use the appropriate techniques for getting any PIP you see into a conversation from Section II "How to Get from Hmmm...TO HIM!" Pay close attention to the chapter "Whad-d'ya-know, Joe?"

Once you find out what he knows about, use all of the techniques we've been discussing in this chapter. Only, now you're not basing it on what he's doing this weekend. Now it is based on him taking some time to sit down with you and explain the thing he is "in the know" about. If you have any confusion about what I mean, go back and reread "Whad-d'ya-know, Joe?" Remember that your job is to practically invite him to ask you out!

Risky Business

The techniques I have just given you will work in many situations. Of course, there is no one method that will work in all situations. The main thing is to keep the following in your mind when you are trying to get a guy to ask you out: *It is painfully difficult for a man to risk rejection by asking a woman out.* If you keep that in the forefront of your thoughts, you will be able to come up with your own methods of reducing his fear in the moment.

As women, we are so lucky that we don't have to be the ones to stick our necks out and risk our heads being chopped off. The least we can do to help a PIP we are interested in, is to be the first one to let on that we like him. Our risk is not nearly as big as the one he must take.

Of course, not all men shake in their boots at the thought of being turned down by a woman. There's a small percentage of men who have no fear of rejection. These men are the most noticeable because they make the most noise, and are the most obnoxious—like the squeaky wheel, getting the greasiest. They are easy to recognize because they never accept "no" for an answer.

It is easy to begin to lump all men together as though they are all impervious to the word "no." I assure you, however, that for many wonderful men, asking and risking being turned down is worse than not asking at all.

Felicia's Favorites

There are many other ways to let a man know you would say "yes." You will have to be creative and think "on your toes" to work with the situation at hand. Here are some examples that have worked for me. Remember to look at where I am coming from. The following examples are not necessarily meant as advice for you to follow specifically; rather, they are illustrations of the frame of mind I am suggesting.

The Perfect Question

Many times I have asked men with whom I was able to flirt my way into a conversation, "Are you flirting with me?" If you use this one, it is important to have a big (shy-ish) smile on your face when you say it.

This is a great question because no matter what they answer, you get the opportunity to let them know you are interested in them. If they say, "Yes," I say, "Good!" If they say, "No," I say, "Darn!" If they say, "Why, are you flirting with me?" I say, with a big shy smile, "I believe I am." At that point, he will usually either ask me out or let me know how his wife/girlfriend is going to react to this when he tells her.

Have I Got a Girl for You

One time a male client of mine that I was "in like with" asked me if I knew of a nice girl like myself that I could set him up with. That is so frustrating, when a guy you like wants you to get him another girl. Sometimes the guy is trying to let you know he wants a date as a way to find out if you are interested. This tactic often backfires on him though, because the feeling comes over the woman that he has counted her out. (Ladies: If you ever use this method, be careful of that.)

So I said, "I know a girl." He said, "What's she like? What does she look like? How tall is she? What's her personality like?" And so forth. I answered every question by describing myself.

Since he had prefaced his request to be set up with "a girl like you," I was fairly sure I would do. "Then again," I thought, "he could have just been being polite." This way, I could see if he liked my type. If he did not like my type, he could say (without rejecting me personally), "She doesn't really sound like my type."

Instead he said, "Sounds great!" I had wanted to not tell him it was me I was setting him up with. I was just going to show up at the meeting place. But I couldn't help myself. I told him it was me I had in mind. He laughed and said, "That's great, I love it!" We went out for a while and ended up great friends. We remain so to this day.

Jazz It Up

Once at a jazz club, I had been flirting with a handsome fellow across the room. Nobody gets up and walks around at this club, so there was no way I could start a conversation with him. Just as I was leaving, I went over and handed him a note I had written on a cocktail napkin. It said, "You have a nice smile. Call me," and then my name and number. He called the next day and we went out.

If you use this method, I recommend that you be careful not to write anything that could be misconstrued as a sexual invitation. Since the method itself is so forward, you want to do what you can to offset that impression. When you do get together, I would also quickly let him know what to expect from you on the physical front. It's only fair.

Resort to Violence?

Another time there was a guy (a hair client) I was sure was interested in me, but would never ask me out. So, one day as we were saying goodbye, I socked him in the arm and said, "Are you gonna ask me out or what?" He said, "I-um-YES!" After a pause, I said, "Well?!" He said, "Wanna go out?" I said, "Why yes, as a matter of fact, I do. When is good for you?" On the date we were having such a great time, he turned to me and said, "I sure am glad I got up the nerve to ask you out."

Bold Type

I know a really gutsy gal—we will call her Lily. Lily did one that I am trying to get up the nerve to try. She saw this PIP at the mall, walked right up to him, threw her arms around his neck and said, in an excited-to-see-you voice, "JACK!! Hey, it's so good to see—uh-oh, you're not Jack, are you? I'm sorry, I thought you were my favorite old ex-boyfriend." The guy said, "Sorry, I'm not." She smiled and said, "Would you like to be?" They had a great conversation and exchanged phone numbers. They went out and had a great time together, though in the end, they were not a match.

JACK!

Shoot Straight

A few times I have tried the straight-out statement, "If you asked me out, I would say 'yes.'" It didn't work. The PIP felt put on the spot, which he didn't like. Also, it made him feel like he was being manipulated into asking me out. My guess is that if you are going to be that bold, it's better to be totally straightforward and ask him out.

Yes, you could just avoid all these shenanigans by doing just that (asking him out). All of this advice is to help you if you are too shy to do that—or if you think being that forward would throw him off or turn him off.

Many men would react that way. Women asking men out often throws off either the man or the woman, or both. Most people are just more comfortable with the traditional roles. However, I do know of several very happy relationships where the woman asked the man first.

Note once again that I am not suggesting that you throw yourself at men. Desperation stinks, and men can smell it a mile away. The difference lies in where you are truly coming from. You must really believe in your own value and therefore not become attached to the result. You are basically interviewing him to see if one of the qualities he possesses is the ability to also see your value! If he does not want to go out with you, then he flunked the interview—therefore you would not go out with him.

Con-grad-uations

(Note: If you replace all of the "you's" in this section with "I," and the "your's" with "my," the following makes an incredible affirmation! Try it.)

So, now you (I) know how to make eye contact in any situation. In your (my) arsenal, you've (I've) got "16 ways to Sunday," to start a conversation with any PIP, anywhere, anytime. You know every trick in the book to keep the "convo" going and move it towards a date. You know how to "target your market" and how to "serve with style" on the "dating court."

You are affirming and creating wonderful quality men everywhere you go. You have opened your mind and heart again—overcome your fears (or at least moved them to simmer on the back burner). You are no longer held back by "*pre*-judgmental" thinking or fear of rejection. You are ready, able and willing to take action, and you are attracting only men who like women like you, by always being yourself.

You have developed true inner confidence (do your self-esteem-ups every day!). You are totally approachable and have absolute empathy for what the man is going through. And now you really know how to empower any man (who is even slightly interested in you) to ask you out.

You have now graduated from the Master-Dation academy, and you can call yourself a Master Dater too! Welcome to the club and congratulations! Now, GO GET EM!!!

Message to Men (The Token Male Chapter)

As I was writing this book, there was a thought that kept creeping up on me: Men will have access to this book…They will read it and then they will know my M.O.

At first I thought, "How can I have this book published in some sort of female underground?" I figured I would give it a title like *Twenty-one Ways to Cure a Yeast Infection in the Privacy of Your Own Home.* Yeah, no way a guy would touch that book with a ten-foot pole, even if it were sitting out at some woman's house!

Then I realized that in reality men reading this book would be fantastic for women's love lives. One of the biggest difficulties we *all* experience in getting together with the opposite sex in today's lifestyle is that we are not sure how to appropriately send signals. We are also often clueless to when others are sending us signals. What we need today are some tools (or codes) to help us communicate better with the PIPs (Potentially Interesting Persons) we come across in our daily lives. The techniques in this book should do the trick!

Yes, I encourage men to read this book and give it to their friends too. Men, be aware that much of the advice in this book will work incredibly well for you too. But remember, your role is different from a woman's. I caution you to not be quite as aggressive with women as I am suggesting they be with you. Keep in mind, women were standing on the sidelines before. The idea is to get women onto the court now. So, don't go scaring them back into the stands.

For men, the best part about reading this book is that you will gain a clear understanding of the dilemmas women face. Knowing this will enable you to move what is in her way out of the way. It's similar to how you might try to get the inside scoop on what a potential employer is looking for in an employee before you apply for the job. Then you can show her (or him) how you are the ideal "man for that job." Most of the time men are "way off" about what qualities they possess that will cause women to be the most interested in them.

Decoding Signals

Just think. There could come a day when all a woman has to do to get a guy to ask her out is to use a Master Dating technique on him. If he knows what the techniques are he will immediately know she wants to go out with him. For instance, the question "You look familiar to me, do I look familiar to you?" could become a universal code for "ASK ME OUT!" If you men knew these were signals, we could *all* bypass the does-she-(or he)-like-me confusion and get on to the more fun, will-he-(or she)-go-out-with-me-again confusion. (Sorry, you'll have to wait for the next book for that one.)

The main thing is for you to always be responding to a woman's signals. In order to do that, you will have to be looking closely for what her signals are. Pay close attention to see if a woman's response is one of interest, or of recoiling. If it is the latter, then back off! If you're not sure, just stay put. Hold your ground until you get a clear signal. Take small steps forward until you get a clear signal from her. Contrary to popular belief, "NO" does mean NO! Never ever push yourself onto a woman who has said no, or anything similar to no!

Women always want to let a guy down easy. It is hard for us to point-blank tell a man "Go away!" If a man makes a play for us and we try to let him know that we are not interested, but he just won't "get it," that makes us mad and annoys us. This will ruin your chances with us. Even if we do agree to go out with you on a "pity date," you have lost more than you have gained. We cannot respect you then.

If you make it known that you like a woman, and she subtly lets you know that she is not interested, let go of the idea of you and her together. If there is any chance that this woman will change her mind, your letting go is the best chance of having that happen. We can respect you for that. We may even like you for it, or realize what we are passing up. Important note: If you just act like you are letting go as a ploy, THIS WILL NOT WORK!!! We can feel that.

What's My Line?

Men always ask me, "What is the best opening line to meet a woman?" Well, I can only speak for myself, but I say it's "Hi, how are you?" followed by "I noticed you and would like to meet you. May I introduce myself?" At that point you pay close attention to her body language and voice tone, and respond to it.

If she seems to be closed, backing off or tentative, then you back off. Apologize for being forward, excuse yourself and walk away. You might say, "I didn't mean to come on too strong. It's just that something about you made me want to meet you. I'll go now." Sometimes all a woman needs is to get a sense that you are responding to and respecting her wishes. She may then say something like, "No, that's okay. You just caught me off guard." At that point, she may introduce herself.

If she doesn't introduce herself (or give you some other positive sign that she wants to talk to you), that means she is not interested in you. This doesn't mean that the "line" didn't work. Maybe she is spoken for, or maybe she doesn't feel comfortable meeting a man in that situation. She may have been approached too many times by pushy men who would not take no for an answer. She may just be totally turned off by men approaching her now. Or, sorry to say, it could mean that she just does not like you—in which case no line would have worked.

Men seem to think there is some magic "line" that will automatically make a woman say, "Yes." This is completely untrue. Sometimes, no matter who you are or what you say, a woman will not become interested in you. Other times, you just may not be what she's looking for.

It's always a good idea to make an attempt for a woman you like—give her a clear signal, even ask her out. But if she does not return your feelings, leave her alone. At least you were a gentleman and didn't give her some goofy con-line and turn her off to the entire male population.

Notice that the "line" I gave you is actually not a line at all. Obviously, there was something about her that made you want to meet her, or you wouldn't be looking for a line. Right? If the line I suggested is not real or natural for you, say something that is. Basically you want to find some polite and direct way to say that you would like to meet her, if she would like to meet you. If she does reject you, all of the stuff in the chapter "What If He Still Does Not Ask (or, How to Deal with Rejection)" goes for you too and will be helpful for you in this situation.

Mating Call

So many men ask me, "When is the right time to call a woman?" They ask, "How long should I wait to call so that the woman won't think I'm desperate?" I say to call exactly when you want to call. I know more women who've decided against going out with a guy because he waited *too long* to call than because he called too soon!

Besides, if a woman is going to make a decision about you based on when you call her, isn't it best that your action to reflect the real you? Let me explain. You might not call a woman, even though you really wanted to. If she wished you had, you would then have blown your chance with her, and for a reason that was not even "the way you really are."

Let's say you call a woman right away and she doesn't like that. That is just a clear sign that you and she would be incompatible in regard to how often each of you likes to check in. At least this way, if you blow your chance, you blew it by being who you really are.

My advice to you is the same as my advice to women. Be who you are, and you will end up attracting a woman who is looking for a man like you. See how it works? Plus, we can tell when you are playing a game. I know men hate it when women play mind games. Guess what? We hate it when you do, too. Rest assured if you see this book at a woman's house that you are dating she will not be playing mind games with you.

Bottom Line

Women want to be listened to and really heard, respected and understood. Follow that advice throughout any courtship and continue throughout the relationship. If you do, you will be incredibly successful with women. Both men and women (in other words, all humans) are flawed. Finding the right combination often takes patience, so hang in there.

This book is written by a woman and is directed towards women. Men are invited and encouraged to read it. But please understand, men, that other than the chapter you just read this book was not directed towards you. In other words all statements are written as though the reader were female. Just keep that in mind as you read.

I acknowledge you for taking the time to try to understand what women go through. I hope this book will make a positive difference in your life. I would love to hear feedback from you about this book or any questions or dilemmas you have in regard to dating. So fax, write, call or e-mail me at the addresses listed at the end of the book.

Final Safety Warning

Be sure to read the "Master Date Safely" section towards the beginning of this book. The following is even more serious advice. My goal is to scare you into being safe when you are out there meeting men. I believe that if you take the precautions spelled out here and in the earlier warning, you can be safe and enjoy dating new men.

About "NO"

There is a great book called *The Gift of Fear*, by Gavin De Becker, and I recommend that every woman read it. It teaches you how to prevent becoming a victim of violent crime or of being stalked. One of the really great pieces of advice he gives is this: When you do not want to go out with a guy, say "NO."

Gavin De Becker explains that often women inadvertently and unintentionally do not dissuade potential stalkers. We do this by trying to let men down easy. For instance, if a guy we don't want to date asks us out, we may say "Not now" when we really mean "Never." De Becker says that in this situation we are better off to simply say "No thank you." He advises that we not give reasons, because to men that just seems like we are negotiating or hoping that they will try harder.

The Gift of Fear also talks a lot about how to listen to and trust your gut instincts. I also strongly encourage that. If you get a bad feeling from someone, don't second-guess yourself! Just get away from them fast.

By reading these few paragraphs you cannot get a strong sense of what *The Gift of Fear* has to offer, so go buy that book. It is likely to help keep you out of all kinds of dangerous situations.

Not Scared?

If you think I'm being paranoid, just watch the news any day of the week. There are a lot of freaks and perverts, rapists and murderers out there who set out to take advantage of us and derive pleasure from hurting women.

The nicer a person you are, the harder this will be for you to accept because you cannot relate to the thinking of a sicko. Unfortunately, that is precisely what makes you a good victim. Men who want to hurt women are looking for women who won't see it coming.

Take This Advice!

Please just take this advice and that which is found in Master Date Safely, and be on the safe side. Think of it this way: If I am wrong, you have nothing to lose. Once you have gotten to know the guy, you can tell him all. If, however, I am right and you don't take my advice, you have **EVERYTHING** to lose.

Every hour, 75 women are raped in this country. Do you think any of those women thought that was going to happen to them that day? No, they probably felt as safe that morning as any other day. Taking the advice in this chapter cannot guarantee that you will not become a victim, but it can cut down immensely on the potential risks associated with meeting any new people and allowing them into your life.

Please Master Date SAFELY!!!!!!!!!!!

Outroduction

I want to thank you for taking the time to read my book. I hope that it was valuable for you and will have a positive impact on your life. Remember that everything found within these pages is just one person's opinions. Mine.

I only ask that you take on the parts of what I have said that fit and work for you. Allow those philosophies into your consciousness. Please build on my theories as I have done with others. I would love to hear about any new concepts that you come up with after percolating on those I have outlined in this book.

You are not allowed to use anything that I have written to beat yourself up with! You are not expected to go out into the world and never mess up an opportunity to meet a PIP. Instead, just try to push yourself outside of your comfort zone a little at a time. Then learn from each new experience.

Ninety percent of this book is meant to just soak into your brain. You should not have to try to remember the specific techniques (though it is fine to do that, if that is what works for you). You will most likely just start to find yourself being more open, outgoing, confident and approachable. It may almost feel at times like you are not even trying to do anything differently, you just suddenly seem to be having better luck with men.

The one exception to the above paragraph is the two exercises. Doing these exercises will not come naturally. In fact, most people have a strong resistance to them. If you do them, I guarantee that this book will be twice as effective as it would be if you did not do them. Once you have done them, however, Master Dating will come more naturally to you than you could ever imagine!!!

My last piece of advice is to be good to yourself—pamper yourself, compliment yourself, even hug yourself regularly. Tell you, you love you! Never insult yourself. Always be aware of your strengths and value. And always remember: *The right man for you will love you most for what is most unique about you!* Once he meets you and gets up the nerve (with your help) to ask you out, the right man will not need much convincing to see that you are the one for him.

The trick *is* getting a date with the right man, it's *not* being the right woman. So, don't go changing yourself into what you think men want. Be proud of who you are. Show off who you are, and be approachable so that the right man for you will notice you when he sees you and be able to do his part in getting the two of you together.

Best of luck and everything else!!!!

So, What's Next?

I have several more books hatching inside my brain. I will now outline them for you. My plan is to eventually write all of them. But, I would like to take a vote—I would love your input as to which would be the most timely for you. If you are willing to be a part of this test market, the next section, "Keep in Touch," will explain several ways of getting in touch with me to give me your opinion.

Other possible books (in no particular order):

- *How to Master Date in Public:* Direct suggestions for how to Master Date when you are in specific places and situations. For instance, how to meet PIPs at parties, parks, concerts, sporting events, over the phone, the bank, market, the Internet and many more. You will also learn how to meet quality men in bars. How to be successful with personal ads, dating services and singles groups. Plus how to turn being set up into a "good thing!" With special chapters for singles who have children. And how to risk turning a friend into a lover without losing a friend. We will also cover blind dates. With tons of suggestions of places and activities where you can meet plenty of quality men!
- *The Interview:* This book will go into how to "interview" a date to see if you and he are right for each other. How to get yourself into a calm, confident mindset that will last throughout the date. Including great suggestions of what to do, where to go and conversation topics that allow you to get a better sense of the guy. And tests that naturally show you if this guy is the right guy for you.
- *Answers to the Most Frequently Asked Questions:* This book will be a compilation of the answers to real questions that you fax, write, call or e-mail to me.
- *This is a Break-Up: Do as I Say, and No One Gets Hurt!* This book will outline how to survive and thrive through the experience of being broken up with. We will also go into great detail about how to gracefully end a relationship. How to let a guy down

easy. How to keep a guy who you're not crazy about at arm's length, while still giving him a chance to "grow on you." I want you to know that I have remained friends with almost every guy who I was once in a relationship with. This is possible. And you can do it too!

Please let us know what you would like to read next, and the order after that too.

We would love to have you as a subscriber to our newsletter, *Love Life!* This newsletter is designed to help us single women to stay centered and confident. It is written for women who are open to a relationship but committed to a state of contentment whether we are in a relationship or not. (In other words, we refuse to be desperate!)

Our commitment is to give you a monthly shot of courage, dose of confidence, valuable insight, useful tools, effective techniques and at least 10 good laughs. It will be a quick read, about a half an hour.

There will be articles about how to meet men. Hysterically funny real stories of different ways other women have met men. Entertaining articles about first dates and so forth. Tons of suggestions on how to really *enjoy* the single life. And the advice column, "Dear Gabby." We are devoted to making a huge positive difference in the lives of our subscribers.

You are hereby invited to receive your first newsletter free! Contact us via any of the options spelled out for you in the next section, "Keep in Touch!"

Keep in Touch!

We want to hear from you! We want to hear your comments, questions, problems, quandaries, realizations, breakthroughs and most of all your Master Dating WINS. What worked for you and what did not, any and all feedback you have to offer.

And of course, your vote on which book we should do next.

Any of your correspondence may appear in our newsletter, *Love Life!* (unless you specify that you do not want it to). Please make sure to let us know if you would like us to use a fake name for you if we do use your story or question in the newsletter. If you have writing aspirations, or a good story to tell, or a great suggestion for other single women, we would love for you to contribute your ideas to our newsletter. The newsletter is described in detail in the previous section, "So, What's Next?"

- Please visit our Web Site at www.MasterDating.com
- Or fax me at (818) 885-5203.
- Or call and leave a voice mail message toll-free at 1-877-LOVE LIFE
- Or write to me at
  Felicia Rose Adler
  c/o Fun-Key Concepts
  7657 Winnetka Ave. Suite 330
  Canoga Park, CA 91306

Recommended Reading

People often ask me how I come up with the stuff in my books and seminars. I put everything I see, hear and read, into this blender called my brain. I let it soak in and then I see what pours out. If what pours out makes sense I share it (welcome to my vortex). The following books are some of what went into the blender.

To feed your soul:

Anything written by the author SARK

Succulent Wild Woman
Living Juicy
Inspiration Sandwich
Creative Companion
SARK's Journal and Play Book

By Claude Clement

The Painter and the Wild Swans (parable)

By Paulo Coelho

The Alchemist (powerful parable)

By Mark Victor Hansen and Jack Canfield

Chicken Soup for the Soul (any in the series)
Chicken Soup for the Woman's Soul (especially this one)

To better understand yourself:

By David Richo

Letting the Light Through
How to Be an Adult

By Cat Williford

Awakening Your Modern Goddess

To better understand others:

By Sam Horn

Tongue Fu!® How to Deflect, Disarm, and Defuse Any Verbal Conflict

To give you courage:

By Susan Jeffers, Ph.D.

Feel the Fear and Do it Anyway (read this book!)

By Sam Horn

Concrete Confidence

To better understand the universe, coincidence and destiny:

By James Redfield
The Celestine Prophecy: An Adventure
By Wayne W. Dyer
Manifest Your Destiny
You'll See It When You Believe It
By Jill Spiegel with Joe Brozic
Flirting with Spirituality
By Robert H. Hopcke
There Are No Accidents
By Lewis Thomas
The Lives of a Cell: Notes of a Biology Watcher (fascinating)
By Chellie Campbell
Financial Stress Reduction

Great advice:

By Jill Spiegel
Flirting for Success
By Karen Salmansohn
How to Make Your Man Behave in 21 Days or Less, Using the Secrets of Professional Dog Trainers. (very funny, but also useful info)
By Barbara De Angelis
The Real Rules (I recommend all books written by The Fabulous De Angelis)
By Susan Jeffers, Ph.D.
Flirting from the Heart
By James Malinchak
The Master Networker

To better understand men:

By Deborah Tannen, Ph.D.
You Just Don't Understand

Safety smarts:

By Gavin De Becker
The Gift of Fear: Survival Signals That Protect Us from Violence

Other Books from Blue Sky Marketing Inc.

101 Questions About Santa Claus, with answers accurately recorded by Bob Litak.
Santa answers such puzzling questions as "How are Santa's reindeer able to fly?" and "What if a home has no chimney?"
Hardcover, 128 pages; 5x7, ISBN: 0-911493-23-9

Reflections Of A Small Town Santa, by Bob Litak.
The wonderful story of how trading a briefcase for a Santa sack forever changed the authors life. Soon to be a classic.
Hardcover, 96 pages; 5x7, ISBN: 0-911493-22-0

The Home Owner's Journal: What I Did & When I Did It, by Colleen Jenkins.
The best-selling, easiest-to-use home record keeping book on the market.
Softcover (spiral binding), 136 pages, 6x9, ISBN: 0-911493-11-5

31 Days to RUIN Your Relationship, by Tricia Seymour & Rusty Barrier.
Tongue-in-cheek (reverse psychology) book of laugh-out-loud "affirmations."
Softcover, 80 pages, 6x4, ISBN: 0-911493-21-2

31 Days to INCREASE Your Stress, by Tricia Seymour.
Tongue-in-cheek (reverse psychology) book of laugh-out-loud "affirmations."
Softcover, 80 pages, 6x4, ISBN: 0-911493-19-0

It's So Cold In Minnesota..., by Bonnie Stewart & Cathy McGlynn.
Hilarious, best-selling regional book poking fun at Minnesota winters.
Softcover, 6x4, 96 pages, ISBN: 0-911493-18-2

It's So Cold In Wisconsin..., by Bonnie Stewart & Cathy McGlynn.
Hilarious, new regional book poking fun at Wisconsin winters.
Softcover, 6x4, 96 pages, ISBN: 0-911493-20-4

Vacation Getaway: A Journal for Your Travel Memories.
With 15 pocket pages, it's the best-designed, best valued travel journal on the market.
Softcover (wire spiral binding), 36 pages (including pockets), 5x9, ISBN: 0-9633573-0-1

Money & Time-Saving Household Hints, from The Leader-Post Carrier Foundation.
Over 1,000 clever, useful, and sometimes startling solutions to everyday problems.
Softcover, 128 pages, 6x9, ISBN: 0-911493-15-8

The Weekly Menu Planner & Shopping List.
The simple and easy way to plan your meals and shopping.
52 weekly sheets, 8.5x11, ISBN: 0-911493-05-0

The Bridal Shower Journal.
Keepsake for recording shower gifts & memories. Includes 25 Thank You cards & envelopes.
Sturdy softcover with spiral wire binding, 22 pages (including 6 pockets), 7x10, ISBN: 0-9633573-2-8

Our Honeymoon: A Journal of Romantic Memories.
With 15 pocket pages, it's the best-designed, best valued honeymoon journal on the market.
Softcover (plastic spiral binding), 36 pages (including pockets), 5x9, ISBN: 0-9633573-1-X